MW00781640

Business Guides on the Go

"Business Guides on the Go" presents cutting-edge insights from practi on particular topics within the fields of business, management, a finance. Written by practitioners and experts in a concise and accessib form the series provides professionals with a general understanding an first practical approach to latest developments in business strategy, lead ship, operations, HR management, innovation and technology manag ment, marketing or digitalization. Students of business administration management will also benefit from these practical guides for their futu occupation/careers.

These Guides suit the needs of today's fast reader.

Adam Berg

# Sales on the Go

## The Salesperson's Desk Reference and Formulary for Sales Success

 Springer

Adam Berg
Wayne, NJ, USA

ISSN 2731-4758　　　　　　　　ISSN 2731-4766　(electronic)
Business Guides on the Go
ISBN 978-1-0716-3210-9　　　　ISBN 978-1-0716-3211-6　(eBook)
https://doi.org/10.1007/978-1-0716-3211-6

This Springer imprint is published by the registered company Springer Science+Business Media, LLC, part of Springer Nature.
The registered company address is: 1 New York Plaza, New York, NY 10004, U.S.A.

*To Diane*
*Because you always believed*

# Introduction

Sales is a noble calling.

It is how things get done in the worldwide economy. Convincing people to exchange money for goods and services is not easy; in fact, it is the most difficult aspect of the free enterprise system and most likely why people find it so challenging. Only the lucky few discover a life in Sales is as exciting as it is satisfying.

As a salesman, you are the sharp end of the stick. You can do a lot of things with the sharp end of the stick; you can point the way forward, you can pry open a door, you can poke it in someone's eye, or you can draw a line in the sand. It is because you know what to do with the sharp end of the stick that makes you valuable.

You are this kind of person. You are a breed apart. If you don't love to sell, you will hate this book.

On a side note, the issue of "rejection" in Sales comes up often. Here is how I view "rejection" in a life of sales and selling: When the question of how I deal with all the rejection when I sell my response is: If someone does not want to buy what I am selling, it is not "rejection," it is simply an excuse to call on them another day.

There is no such thing as "no" in sales – only "later."

To be blunt, "rejection" is when your mother says: "Your father is right – you are an idiot. Get out!" That's rejection.

This book was born when I visited a bookstore and a doctor's office in the same day. I went to the section in the bookstore on "Business" and there were hundreds of books on selling, how to sell, how to follow up, how to get the meeting, how to negotiate, how to close, and ultimately the marketing of the product and countless other tomes on how to extract money from strangers in the sales process.

Later that day, in the doctor's office, I noticed he had one book on his desk. It was a pharmacological desk reference, a formulary for drugs. There were no other books around. It was the only book he needed, and it was present and readily at hand to help him do his job on a minute-by-minute basis.

Reflecting on the bookstore visit, it occurred to me there was no such desk reference book for selling. So, I got the idea to write this book in the doctor's office and started writing it later that day.

This book is written for the professional salesperson. Whether the salesperson is starting a career in sales or is a grizzled, experienced, case-hardened one, being aware of, or referring to, the sales and selling basics are requirements for future and/or continued success.

The book is organized in to three sections, with five chapters in each section reflecting on the five basic phases in selling to a buyer, in selling in a marketing environment, and in selling in a management setting. These are:

Selling Section:

1) Cold calling
2) Following up
3) Getting the meeting
4) Negotiating
5) Closing

Marketing Section:

1) Research
2) Strategy
3) Planning

4) Tactics

5) Return on investment

Management Section:

1) Explain

2) Persuade

3) Direct

4) Review

5) Reward

Within each chapter are ten of the most common responses a salesperson will encounter while selling and follow-on explanations as to what the response means, what your response should be, what you mean by the response, will you make a sale, why it happens the way it does, and whether you should consult with your Boss. (More on the Boss, and other Players, below.)

Each one is on a separate page, is short and to the point. It will help you forecast, recognize, anticipate, and engage with the most common objections, rejections, and excuses you hear every day. You will develop the skills needed to meet and overcome these objections to your advantage no matter what you sell, or where, or to whom.

## How to Use This Book

In your role as Salesperson, you will find this book useful under the following circumstances and conditions:

You have something to sell, a product or concept. You have reached the sales prospect and are not talking to, or trying to circumvent, a gatekeeper such as an Executive Assistant. You are using a headset. Ditch your telephone handset or mobile phone speaker setting. You need your hands to be free to take notes and look up phrases in this book. For best sales results, you need the person you are selling to in your head, and the best way to get a person into your head is to put them directly in your ear.

You are alone, or in an environment where the buyer cannot see you using the book. If possible, keep the book out of view during video conferences.

You will have the pertinent section open when the call is made, so access to the responses can be found swiftly. That is why the chapter headings are repeated at the beginning of each chapter.

A pen that works, preferably two. An 8½" by 11" yellow lined pad, nothing smaller, ever. You lose smaller pieces of paper, and they are hard to file.

This book is meant to be used in real-time situations. It should be always on the desk and referred to constantly. As with most skills, intellectual or athletic, routine, and disciplined practice of fundamentals leads to superior results. Champions, leaders, and winners always practice the basics of their chosen endeavor and refer to the simple truths of what they do and how they do it even in the most complex situations.

However, 99% of situations faced in life are neither complex nor mysterious. You, the Salesperson, have seen these situations, and dealt with them before. Remembering and applying the foundations of our craft are keystones to our success.

Now, go get 'em!

# The Salesperson's Mantras

"Try" is not a <u>tactic</u>
"Could" is not a <u>goal</u>
"Luck" is not an <u>asset</u>
"Wish" is not a <u>doctrine</u>
"Assume" is not a <u>theory</u>
"Probably" is not a <u>vision</u>
"Believe" is not a <u>strategy</u>
"Maybe" is not an <u>outcome</u>
"Should" is not a <u>commitment</u>
<u>and</u>
"Never Need What You Want, and Never Want What You Need"
<u>and</u>
"The Simple Truth Is the Truth Is Always Simple"
<u>and</u>
"The Devil Is Never Ugly"

# The Salesperson's Mantras Explained

The genesis of the first Mantra was a spasmodic reaction to the toneless droning of an executive who was desperately working to explain to a client why something he was responsible for had not materialized.

In one long sentence, he used most of the quoted words in this Mantra, and then in another sentence, as the sweat was pouring through his shirt when he realized the client was not impressed with his meager excuse, he used the rest of the words.

The sentence went something like this: "We were **trying** to get things done so we **could** generate some **luck**, which is better than having some **hope** in this situation if we did not want to **assume** that **probably** we would have to re-think our approach."

This sentence was a prime example of waffling and explaining why something did not work, or did not happen, instead of offering a conclusive summary of what did or did not happen.

The vernacular of selling leaves little wiggle room for fudging results if you want to be convincing.

After the meeting I re-constructed all the wiggle room words I could remember, then equated them to the actions or results the executive had sought to communicate.

As a Salesperson, avoid these wiggle room words at all costs. If you are using them now in your sales efforts, stop. If you write them in an email, letter, memo, or text, use a thesaurus and find the action word you need.

xiv The Salesperson's Mantras Explained

If you hear them, discount them, and judge the person using them accordingly. Finally, if this really strikes a chord in you, and you use these words often, then you will find going cold turkey harder than anything you have ever tried to stop doing.

### "Never Need What You Want and Never Want What You Need"

This Mantra is the "Sweet Spot" in negotiating. You cannot negotiate anything if you need what the other person has so badly that you will give up anything for it. You cannot negotiate anything if you want what the other person has so badly that you will accept anything offered for it. Learn to walk away and learn to let the other person walk away.

### "The Simple Truth Is the Truth Is Always Simple"

This Mantra is a good thing to live life by. The truth is never complicated, which is why it is intrinsically linked to insight.

### "The Devil Is Never Ugly"

This Mantra applies to life in general not just Sales. That which is tempting is never unbecoming or repulsive. No one has a hankering for uncooked rice. No one is addicted to jet lag. In sales, a salesperson can be fooled, and efforts derailed, if the salesperson is distracted by false objectives because they are tempting or attractive. These false goals are usually associated with short-term gain, or an advantage seized at the expense of someone else; neither of which is healthy behavior nor resulting in maximum long-term benefit.

# Notes on This Book

## The Format

You will recognize the format in this book as "role-playing." In my opinion, "role-playing" is the oldest and most common sales training tool ever devised. I have been in role-playing scenarios since my first job. It was likely invented when first salesperson heard the first objection and enlisted a fellow salesperson to create guided conversations to help identify common issues and how to solve them.

There is no magic to sales just like there is no magic in role playing. This book simply refines an old age technique.

## The Settings

This book is written to address a universe of applications. The book is not particular to, or specific for, any business, industry, sector, company, corporation, organization, product, service, or person. It is about nothing, and about everything. It is portable, adaptable, and malleable and suitable for all types of sales environments. It is unalloyed, non-partisan, without prejudice, non-allied or oriented to any direction, outlook, or point of view. That is why nothing is identifiable is in here. You can find these situations nowhere, everywhere, and at any point in time.

## The Spoken Word

I cannot recall where I have heard the phrases you will read about and respond to. I cannot recall who said them, where, why, in what context, in what setting, which location in time, space, or otherwise. I cannot put faces with phrases. All I can tell you is I know I heard them.

**The Players:**

**You** – obviously.

**Buyer** – The person you are responding to in the Sales Section.

**Marketer** – The person you are responding to in the Marketing Section.

**Manager** – The person you are responding to in the Management Section.

**Boss** – Your supervisor, or someone you trust that you work with, that you report to, or have reported to, or someone who is mentoring you. Someone who likes you and will look out for you. Someone indispensable.

## A Note on Pronouns and Attributions

To keep things simple, I've adopted a gender-neutral style and will say "they" or "them". I do not say "the Buyer" or "the Manager will show you that…" I simply say "Buyer will say this" or "Marketer wants to point out…"

**A note on location as it relates to the author:**

I was born in New York City and have spent my sales career largely in North America. Therefore, my cultural orientation and the language, attitudes, dispositions, emotional, and logical responses are cooked in the stew of this geographical sales cauldron. While I have been lucky to do considerable amounts of selling internationally, I have learned a lot from this experience and am lucky to have it; it rounds out my perspective, but ultimately, this is an American speaking.

**When I got started:**

I made my first sale when I was 12 years old; loved it and never looked back. This book is based on things I have heard since then. You don't want to know how long that is.

What is said to you in response your first contact?
What does what is said to you really mean?
What do you say in response that shows you understand?
What do you really mean when you respond?
What are the next steps?
What are the chances of you making the sale?
Should you confer with your Boss?
Now, for the first time, presented in a real-time format you can use as the conversation unfolds, is the sales process stripped of all the trappings and hidden meanings.
Use this book to decode the sales process and demonstrate that you:
Understand.
Cannot be fooled.
Can overcome any objection.
Can deal with, handle, and turn to your advantage anything said to you.
And get the sale!

---

This book will make clear, how to deal with, and overcome, the most common responses you will hear in a sales career.

# Contents

## Part II    The Marketing Section

## Part III    The Management Section

# Part I

## The Sales Section

This section is about selling whatever it is you are selling to Buyer.

In your sales career this will be the most straightforward interaction you will have because your relationship with the buyer is simple;

**Buyer's job is to not spend money on whatever it is you are selling.**

It would seem to be the opposite; Buyer's job is to spend money to acquire things that advance Buyer's interests.

Buyer wants to spend as little as possible on your product while the organization Buyer works for sells the most of what it has on hand. That way, Buyer increases the spread between what Buyer has in the budget to spend and what the organization can convince Buyer to spend on what the organization is selling. This increases profits beyond the profit margin represented by the cost to make, or acquire, the product and for what the product sells.

Which is also why you will hear the things you hear. Each comment is a way for Buyer to judge where you, and your product, fit on Buyer's scale of what Buyer must have, would like to have, can decide later about, or pass.

You have heard of "active listening" and "mirroring" as sales techniques? Forget it. Buyer will pick up on the fact that you are using these techniques and immediately show you the door figuratively or literally.

I think "active listening" and "mirroring" were invented by someone who does not sell. They are phrases in search of a context.

My perspective on listening and hearing is listening is not hearing and hearing is not listening. The simple fact of listening is you cannot listen if you are talking. So, if you want to listen, stay quiet. If you want to hear someone, make sure you understand what they are saying and if you do not, ask intelligent questions when it is your turn to speak.

Some Buyers are better at this than others. Some are more transparent than others. Some should never be Buyers. Always keep in mind Buyers are just people. Heaven knows what they think about you, so always be kind, patient, considerate, professional, and calm.

The Sales Section will outline situations and as you will see you will have to make your own assessment about each Buyer, what they say, how they say it, and what you will do next.

When you sell, you are always in control.

# 1

# Cold Calling

**Buyer says:**

1) "It's never a good time but go ahead."
2) "Actually…." (anything that follows this is useless)
3) "That's not what we do but send me your materials anyway."
4) "We don't have any money."
5) "We have had experience with this, and it's not for us."
6) "We don't want to be in that business."
7) "No thanks, we're not interested."
8) "I will take it to my Marketing/Sales/Management Department and get back to you."
9) "Call me back later today."
10) "I am always happy to listen – what's on your mind?"

© Results Through Focus, LLC 2023
A. Berg, *Sales on the Go*, Business Guides on the Go,
https://doi.org/10.1007/978-1-0716-3211-6_1

**Preparing for Cold Calling – Three things you need to have before you start:**

1) A prospect list to include:

a. Name
b. Company
c. Title
d. Email (if you can find it)
e. Phone number with area code
f. Time zone (Don't call PST at 9am EST!)

Why? You want to work the list like a shopping list – clear and concise. Don't fumble around for the next call – have it ready to go.

2) Pen and paper at the ready.
  Why? You don't want to scrounge around for a piece of paper and a pen when you start listening. The Buyer can hear if you are not ready to sell – and so, no sale!

3) A place with no distractions.

Why? Working in an "Open Plan" environment? Find a quiet place even if it is a stairwell. Extraneous noise makes it sound like you are calling from an engine room in a submarine.

Sell peer to peer, not ear to ear.

## The Situation: Cold Calling

**Buyer**: "It's never a good time but go ahead."

**Buyer means:** I am a polite individual who has common courtesy enough to listen to anyone that can put two words together. You have less than thirty seconds to get my attention, however, after that if this is not of interest, I will go to my next stock phrase and end the conversation.

**What you say:** "I appreciate the time, and I will get right to the point."

**You mean:** Pal, I know the clock is running and you gave me thirty seconds. You can count on me to dispense with any preliminaries and get right to the point as to why I am going to ask you to give me money.

**Why this happens:** Buyer's opening line is a poor attempt at humor to break the ice. After you have said "have I caught you at a bad time" Buyer acknowledges that time is the currency you both traffic in and turns it into a joke and a bad one at that. However, it does mean Buyer is sympathetic to your situation and has either been in your shoes or is genuinely interested in talking to strangers.

**Is this a good sign that you will make a sale:** Yes.

**What you do:** Look at your watch and go for it. End your first sentence in thirty seconds or less and invite comment.

**Boss?** No. You are well on your way and have nothing to report at this juncture in the sales process. This is a routine circumstance.

## The Situation: Cold Calling

**Buyer:** "Actually…." (anything that follows this is useless.)

**Buyer means:** I am not the right person, but I don't want to hang up on you. I will help get you to the next stop, but it may not be the right stop, but at least you will no longer be my problem, and I can't be criticized if you turn out to be selling the biggest product of the season.

**What you say:** "I completely understand, thank you for pointing me in the right direction".

**What you mean:** Thank you for not hanging up on me.

**Why this happens:** "Actually" is the new Americanism for "not my job." "I am not the person, this is not my department, you have the right company but not the right division" – take your pick. This person works in a big organization where they are constantly covering their behinds. It is vital that you are not dismissed because you could be valuable, but Buyer does not have the time, interest, or inclination to qualify you further. Buyer will foist you off on a colleague, but Buyer can't be faulted because it wasn't Buyer's decision to either buy or dismiss your product.

**Is this a good sign that you will make a sale?** Yes.

**What you do:** Thank Buyer for the precise information about who to speak to next. That way you have another lead and be happy. Then, make a mental note that Buyer was as helpful as possible for that person to be in that circumstance.

**Boss?** Yes, inform Boss you have a new lead as a referral from a dead prospect.

## The Situation: Cold Calling

**Buyer:** "That's not what we do but send me your materials anyway."

**Buyer means:** I don't have the time or inclination to tell you flat out that I am not interested, and you are wasting your time because that is not how I am constituted, and our corporate culture abhors commitment to a position. Therefore, I will hedge my bet, and when you send me your materials I will either dump it off to someone down the hall or line my bird cage with it.

**What you say:** "Thank you for the clarification and we will be in touch soon."

**What you mean:** I won't waste the postage or the electricity for the internet.

**Why this happens:** Today, people have little or no idea how to be direct, to the point, or declarative. It is better to let someone know up front if you are interested, or to what degree you may be interested, rather than dither. It is better to be transparent when you are dedicated to not wasting time.

**Is this a good sign that you will make a sale?** No.

**What you do:** Make note of Buyer in your database and follow-up in ninety days. When you call back, ask for that Buyer by name. If Buyer is there, don't bother talking to Buyer, call back in another ninety days. Keep this up until Buyer has left the company or someone has taken Buyer's place. This kind of attitude on Buyer's part is a total non-starter and over time most likely will result in Buyer's termination for being ineffectual. Find someone else in the company or find a new Buyer.

**Boss?** No. Just another day in Sales. You are expected to deal with it.

## The Situation: Cold Calling

**Buyer:** "We don't have any money."

**Buyer means:** We don't have any money for your project.

**What you say:** "That's not a problem, I can work with that."

**What you mean:** We both know if you had no money we would not be talking. Therefore, please allow me a minute to communicate the value of what I have to sell, and we can place a monetary value on it when we are done discussing it.

**Why this happens:** Using the excuse "they have no money" is a blanket phrase that gets Buyer out of the sales equation as quickly as possible by dismissing the merits of your product without having to contemplate its value.

**Is this a good sign that you will make a sale?** Yes.

**What you do:** Break through this common barrier and start a discussion of the pros and cons of the product you are selling. Take money out of the conversation by saying "what if it didn't cost you anything, or you had all the money in the world. Let's discuss this based on its pure merit as a product."

**Boss?** No. Not for office discussion. But a good "war story" over drinks.

## The Situation: Cold Calling

**Buyer:** "We have had experience with this, and it's not for us."

**Buyer means:** I have a blanket approach to anything new that smacks of something I have seen previously even though you and I both know that what you have is only remotely similar. However, I cannot be bothered to think now and furthermore since this is familiar to me, I am covered in saying "no" to you because of our previous review of a generally similar product.

**What you say:** "That's interesting. Please tell me about that prior experience."

**What you mean:** Let me hear about the product you rejected before so I can contrast and compare mine to that one and point out the benefits that I have to offer seeing how you were so rude and closed minded that I could not even get to that part of my pitch.

**Why this happens:** This response is always made by someone who has a hair trigger response to strategic situations. People who shoot from the hip are always certain of their aim, and often miss their mark.

**Is this a good sign that you will make a sale?** Yes.

**What you do:** You are forced in this situation to work within the confines of Buyer's mindset and orientation to things that are new and novel. Expanding Buyer's thinking must take place on Buyer's terms and inside the boundaries of Buyer's prior experience. This can be accomplished by having Buyer tell the tale of prior experience and how Buyer found its faults, how Buyer saved the company tons of money, staved off disaster and was the hero. Once that story is told and Buyer is satisfied you are sufficiently cowed by Buyer's toughness, ask what would have had to be different about that product for it to be attractive. Take Buyers' responses and match them to your product's attributes.

**Boss?** No. This is a routine counter-objection tactical approach.

## The Situation: Cold Calling

**Buyer:** "We don't want to be in that business."

**Buyer means:** Buyer may indeed not be in that business. Or Buyer may say that as a dodge.

**What you say:** "It's my error then, apologies, I will check my files. But what business are you in exactly —my files are usually fully accurate."

**What you mean:** If you really are not in the business category I am selling into then I will get off the phone immediately. If you are trying to stave me off with this simple answer you give all the salespeople, then I need to find out why you don't want to hear what I have to say.

**Why this happens:** Momentum. Buyer has to answer so many unsolicited calls daily that Buyer denies access to the decision-making apparatus in Buyer's organization by stating they are not in the business you are looking for. That way, Buyer figures Buyer can take the personality issue out of the sales equation, or any other factor – such as Buyer may not be the right person, or you may have not reached the right department. Or Buyer could not be in the business in the first place. Sometimes "what it is" is 'what it is."

**Is this a good sign that you will make a sale?** No.

**What you do:** Selling in this instance is a brutal uphill climb. Qualify the situation as to what business Buyer really is in, and move on to a new prospect, or move to qualify interest quickly. If Buyer is hiding true interest, you will have to uncover it at that moment or Buyer will dismiss you. These kinds of people are not conversationalists.

**Boss?** Yes. Ask Boss if Boss has had previous experience with this company.

## The Situation: Cold Calling

**Buyer Says:** "No thanks, we're not interested."

**Buyer means:** Can you hear the door slamming in your face?

**What you say:** "I'm confused Buyer; in what are you not interested?"

**What you mean:** I do hear the door slamming in my face, but I am sticking my proverbial foot in the door before the door reaches my face. Please engage me in conversation so I can ignite an interpersonal rapport which leads to better outcomes than this wholly unsatisfactory dumpster fire of a mess so far.

**Why this happens:** As this is the most common catch-all of phrases designed to end business conversations there are limitless numbers of reasons why it happens. Someone could be too busy, too distracted to listen, to make a judgement, too bored, too upset with a bad day, or genuinely not interested. The "why" of "why this happens" in this case is irrelevant, that it happens often, is. How you deal with this one phrase over time will determine to a large extent how good a salesperson you are.

**Is this a good sign that you will make a sale?** Yes.

**What you do:** Get Buyer to say one more word. Then you say two words, and get Buyer to say three, and so on. Think of building your conversation as an upside-down pyramid, with Buyer's first word as the bottom block, and your next two words the second row, Buyer's next three the third row and so on. Eventually you will have a real dialogue going and

Buyer will forget Buyer ever said Buyer was not interested. In fact, Buyer may not even recall Buyer said it, or the basis of Buyer's initial rebuff of your sales advance.

**Boss?** Yes. But tell Boss you used this technique only if you close the sale.

## The Situation: Cold Calling

**Buyer** "I will take it to my Marketing/Sales/Management Department and get back to you."

**Buyer means:** I can't make the decision as to "yes" or "no," so I am going to put some more eyeballs on it, if and when I can raise the subject without attracting too much attention, if I can remember to do it at all, and if I forget to raise the point in the next meeting with the group I won't bring it up until the Sun goes supernova, so don't hold your breath, and furthermore if I do get some kind of answer, which most likely won't be a "yes," then getting back to you will be way down on the list of the many things I have to do, all of which are more important than your situation.

**What you say:** "That's great! Thank you for seeing the merit in the product. When will we know more?"

**What you mean:** By saying "we" you invest Buyer in your process, and you have made Buyer at best an ally and at worst an accomplice. The point here is not to know when, or what group is analyzing the sale, the point here is to get Buyer to work for your project on the inside of Buyer's organization. Right at this juncture, you must feed Buyer every reason why Buyer wants to champion the project in the company once you hang up the phone.

**Why this happens:** In many cases you will encounter someone who sees the merit of the product you are selling, and can even be enthusiastic about it, but Buyer works in an organization that has a procedure, practice, and protocol for bringing new ideas forward. You must recognize this, embrace it, acknowledge it, understand how it works, be patient with it and then give Buyer all the tools Buyer needs to pry things forward towards the sale.

**Is this a good sign that you will make a sale?** Yes.

**What you do**: Simply ask what else Buyer needs to go on in the process. Do not ask anything about who Buyer is going to or when or how they work. Then tell Buyer when Buyer will have the extra materials. By email? Immediately. Any other items must arrive by the next day. Buyer will tell you when to follow-up and if Buyer does not, don't ask, just make a note to call in eight days. Most new business meetings happen every week.

**Boss?** No. This is routine.

## The Situation: Cold Calling

**Buyer:** "Call me back later today."

**Buyer means:** Exactly that. Call Buyer back later today.

**What you say:** Thank you. My name is….and I will call you later." Hang up.

**What you mean:** Buyer, thank you for not hanging up on me. I respect your polite but direct command and will comply without further comment.

**Why this happens:** "Call me back later today" is a neutral response to an incoming phone call from anyone Buyer does not have to report to. Take it for what it is and do not read anything into it; it is not a code. Furthermore, this is a different response from "It's never a good time but go ahead" (see above) because the former is an order to call back, the latter is a common but poor attempt at humor that gives you a small window to speak.

**Is this a good sign that you will make a sale?** Yes.

**What you do:** Hang up and call back later in the day. Make sure you give Buyer your name as a tactic for you to use when you call back. You can remind Buyer you called earlier, and your name was (…). If you make the call before lunch, wait one hour after a typical lunch break, and then place the call, but never within one hour of 5pm. If you make the original call after 2pm, wait until the next morning at least one hour after a typical opening time in that industry. Buyer may or may not remember you, so be patient.

**Boss?** No. This is just a phone call situation.

## The Situation: Cold Calling

**Buyer:** "I am always happy to listen – what's on your mind?"
**Buyer means:** I can give you about 60 seconds, but during those 60 seconds I will listen.
**What you say:** "Excellent. I will get right to the point."
**What you mean:** I recognize you are giving me the gift of time. Therefore, I will not abuse it with preamble or discourse. In sixty seconds, you will have enough information to make an informed decision as to whether you would like to hear more.
**Why this happens:** It is likely you are talking to another Salesperson who has sold in your position and pays it forward. This is a gentleperson with manners and respect for strangers doing a job for a living.
**Is this a good sign that you will make a sale?** Yes
**What you do**: Time is money. That is Buyer's polite message. Buyer is giving you time, so you give Buyer the opportunity to make money. Do not mistake Buyer's first response as an invitation to chat. Get to the selling proposition and let it hang. You must present the sales equation in less than sixty seconds or time will lapse. If that happens, Buyer will quickly, firmly, but very politely, end the call.
**Boss?** Yes. This is a good situation to remind Boss you know what you are doing.

# 2

# Following Up

**Buyer says:**

1) "Yes, I got the materials, but I have not looked at them yet."
2) "Yes, I looked at the materials, but I am not the right person. I passed along to...."
3) "I got it and shared it with my associates. It's interesting, can you tell me more?"
4) "We reviewed the materials, and we will pass. Thank you."
5) "I don't know what to think. The materials arrived, and I was waiting for your call."
6) "I see how we can use your product, and I am checking with some customers to see if it works with them. I'll get back to you in a week or so."
7) "We've looked at it, but we don't know what to do with it."
8) "It's opportune you contacted us. We would like to explore terms; what do you suggest?"
9) "I got your materials. Can I call you right back?"
10) "I have a lot on my calendar right now."

© Results Through Focus, LLC 2023
A. Berg, *Sales on the Go*, Business Guides on the Go,
https://doi.org/10.1007/978-1-0716-3211-6_2

**Preparing for Following Up: Three things you need to have before you start:**

1) Your calendar, or follow-up Sales Management Software open to the day you are calling. You cannot follow-up effectively without a plan, and your plan starts with your follow-up list. This is like the prospect list, but it has been worked, at least once.
2) Open your email to your ""Sent Mail" window so you can see exactly what you said and to whom.
3) A good mouse. You will be toggling between the Sales Management software and your Sent emails, so be sure you have either a good touch pad, mouse, or touch screen. Keep the grease from breakfast or lunch or snacks off the touch pad, keep the batteries fresh in the mouse and clean the touch screen according to the manufacturer's instructions.

# The Situation: Following Up

**Buyer Says:** "Yes, I got the materials, but I have not looked at them yet."

**Buyer means:** The materials landed on my desk. I glanced at them and they are in a pile of things to review when I have the time, which is rarely, the interest, which is fleeting, the energy to wrestle with a new concept, which is low, and the will-power, which is weak, to run with something someone is trying to sell to me and bring it forward to my company for incorporation into our day-to-day existence, which is my most precious resource and key to my advancement and/or survival.

**What you say:** "That they arrived is a great start! When do you think you can give it some consideration, or if you have looked at them briefly, do you have any first thoughts?"

**What you mean:** I know you have them, and I am going to have you live up to your thin commitment to me when we first spoke that you would review the sales proposition.

**Why this happens:** Buyer does not want to sound like an idiot (see next entry) and admit Buyer did not get the materials but needs time to give you a next step if there is one.

**Is this a good sign that you will make a sale?** Yes.

**What you do**: Firmly establish a next follow-up day and time, and then contact the Buyer exactly then, without fail. Send an immediate follow-up reiterating when you will contact Buyer. Immediately means immediately, not later that day, not in an hour; hang up and send the email. Then move on to the next situation in your day.

**Boss?** No. This is routine, it takes practice to send the email immediately, but no need to tell Boss you practice.

## The Situation: Following Up

**Buyer Says:** "Yes, I looked at the materials, but I am not the right person. I passed them along to…."

**Buyer means:** I was not interested enough to champion the project forward in the organization. If I were enthusiastic, I would have told you so and said I passed the materials along with a recommendation or felt there was a need for what you have and that we should look at it seriously. This response above is worse than a wet, dead fish handshake.

**What you say:** "I appreciate your interest and support. Would it be best to follow-up with you, or can you tell me who I should contact next and when would be a good time to do that?"

**What you mean:** Under no circumstances will I contact you again, but I said it to be polite. You will give me the follow-up name, or I will pry it out of you, or will contact your company again in a week and start from the beginning. You know it, and Buyer knows it, and Buyer will be relieved to give you the next name.

**Why this happens:** Organizational inertia is the biggest impediment to productivity in this country. You are facing it here. It is easier to do no business than some business.

**Is this a good sign that you will make a sale?** No.

**What you do:** Get the next name and don't get off the phone until you do. Expend all your political capital with this Buyer getting the name. If getting the name was easy, ask when it would be a suitable time to follow-up. If that information is forthcoming, engage in general conversation about how the next step will work, who the next contact is and how best to proceed. If getting the next contact's name was hard, thank the Buyer and move on.

It is vital you contact the next person immediately before your first Buyer can muddy or poison the waters by contacting the next person before you. Hang up the phone, pick up the phone, and re-dial.

**Boss?** No. You don't have anything to report because until you contact the new Buyer, you are treading water.

## The Situation: Following Up

**Buyer Says:** "We reviewed the materials, and we will pass. Thank you."

**Buyer means:** No means no.

**What you say:** "I appreciate your time. Was there something about the product I could change to make you reconsider?"

**What you mean:** I respect your position and will take the "no" as a "no" unless you engage me in conversation, in which case "no" may not be a "no."

**Why this happens:** Some Buyers know what they are doing and know what they want. These people are excellent Buyers because they will not waste time.

**Is this a good sign that you will make a sale?** No.

**What you do**: Gauge the response. If Buyer does not engage in conversation the "no" is a solid "no." Thank Buyer, make a note in your files to keep this person as a Buyer for the next project, and move on. This is a good Buyer.

**Boss?** No. As above, move on.

## The Situation: Following Up

**Buyer Says:** "I got it and shared it with my associates. It's interesting, can you tell me more?"

**Buyer means:** I read it over and over and have found at least one way I can use it. However, I need to know more about what it is going to cost me to buy it. Buyer does not want you to tell Buyer more about the product, Buyer is asking obliquely what it costs. Buyer does this so as not to encourage you or have you pressure Buyer.

**What you say:** "Of course and thank you. There are (pick a number less than four because no one believes there are ever more than three good reasons for anything in life) main attributes to the product I can go over with you, and why specifically these were tailored to your company."

**What you mean:** I am not going to tell you the cost because you did not ask. I am going to extol virtues of the product in answer to your question.

**Why this happens:** The person doing the buying never wants to be the first person in the conversation to raise the issue of cost.

**Is this a good sign that you will make a sale?** Yes.

**What you do**: Give Buyer the less than four attributes of the product even if they are retreads of the attributes which are right in front of Buyer. Pretend the product has no cost, or you have not decided on a price. Reiterate how, before you sent the proposal or made the call, you custom tailored the product to suit needs you had detected as a good Salesperson. After you have done this, wait for the response. Don't raise the price issue until or unless, prompted.

**Boss?** Yes. Go over the pricing to make sure Boss knows you got into a discussion about pricing and how you are moving to a close the deal.

## The Situation: Following Up

**Buyer Says:** "I don't know what to think. The materials arrived, and I was waiting for your call."

**Buyer means:** Explain why your sales proposition is relevant to me but I was not interested enough, or too lazy, to contact you first.

**What you say:** "I would be delighted to help you. Would this be an opportune time to talk about it, or should I call you back?"

**What you mean:** I can help you see why I contacted you, or I can give you the "out" to forward me to another Buyer who may be in a better position to understand, or act on, the sales proposition.

**Why this happens:** People are confused when confronted with variables, especially those that are not home grown, or out of the norm.

**Is this a good sign that you will make a sale?** No.

**What you do**: Give Buyer the simplest but most potent answer you can develop. In any event you should have this phrase or sentence at the ready, so it is not a surprise to have to use it. If that does not ignite understanding the next step is re-qualify Buyer as the right person to talk to. If Buyer is the right person, then continue to engage in conversation.

**Boss?** No. Boss will find this merry-go-round boring.

## The Situation: Following Up

**Buyer Says:** "I see how we can use your product, and I am checking with some customers to see if it works with them. I'll get back to you in a week or so."

**Buyer means:** If I can get monetary support downstream in my sales cycle, there will be a place for your product in my organization and I will pay you for it. Sit tight and don't bother me for at least two weeks.

**What you say:** "Excellent! Is there more I can provide you with now, or should we just talk later when you have the data?"

**What you mean:** I acknowledge you see the utility in what I am selling, you know what you are doing, I am offering more details to help you sell, and I won't bother you for two weeks, but after that I will call you.

**Why this happens:** Your Buyer can buy, but because Buyer is a competent executive, Buyer has to make sure Buyer's cost to buy the product from you can be recouped when Buyer's organization uses your product and Buyer needs to check with colleagues about this important issue. Buyer needs time and space to make it happen.

**Is this a good sign that you will make a sale?** Yes.

**What you do**: Take Buyer's lead. If Buyer needs more materials send them. If not, don't press. Wait two weeks, then follow-up. This is a good Buyer.

**Boss?** No, not at this juncture. But if you close, then tell Boss the sequence of events. Boss will think you a genius warrior and buy you a cup of coffee from the office coffee machine.

## The Situation: Following Up

**Buyer Says:** "We've looked at it, but we don't know what to do with it."

**Buyer means:** Your product has merit but presents risks to us. Until you tell me how you think I should use it, I won't tell you I am interested. I need to have a conversation with you about how to solve internal problems that affect your sale, but which you had no idea existed when you contacted us.

**What you say:** "That's a common reaction to this excellent product I have for you. It's so good it can be used any number of ways. Tell me more about your situation and let's go from there."

**What you mean:** You are telling Buyer they are not alone, and it is okay for Buyer not to be able to see clearly all the way to closing on the deal in the first conversation.

**Why this happens:** A typical Buyer in the middle or upper-middle ranks of an organization cannot commit the company to the sale at this stage, even if your product is the answer to their prayers. They must insert a middle, qualifying step. Buyer having this conversation with colleagues is this middle step.

**Is this a good sign that you will make a sale?** Yes

**What you do:** Go with the flow. Answer every question, and then ask for a meeting or a next phone call to discuss specific action steps and/or terms.

**Boss?** Yes. Ask Boss to join you on the next call. The next few steps to closing based on this situation are tiny, dicey steps. Good to have Boss help you here.

## The Situation: Following Up

**Buyer Says:** "It's opportune you contacted us. We would like to explore terms; what do you suggest?"

**Buyer means:** We are ready to talk about money. Please provide the opening gambit.

**What you say:** "That is great news. I will prepare proposed preliminary terms and send them to you immediately. After you get them, when would it be appropriate for me to follow-up?"

**What you mean:** Because you have given me the gift of a sale with so little fuss and bother, it is incumbent upon me to make the next move and propose specific costs. This may put me at an initial disadvantage, but this is the quid pro quo I must provide because this sale moved along so quickly.

**Why this happens:** Your Buyer can make things happen and does not want to waste time. Buyer wants to see what it will cost.

**Is this a good sign that you will make a sale?** Yes.

**What you do:** While this circumstance happens the least of the ten most common follow-up situations, it does happen. It can take you by surprise, but don't let on that it does. You are so ready for a long slog that when the doors open effortlessly, you can be caught flat-footed. Take the response in stride, like it happens every day, and put forward your best, fairest deal. Of course, this is a good Buyer.

**Boss?** No. Write up the deal, get it signed, get the money. Let Boss find out from the Accounting Department that the money arrived.

## The Situation: Following Up

**Buyer Says:** "I got your materials. Can I call you right back?"

**Buyer means:** I am too busy right now to talk. I may or may not remember to call you back, may or may not have your number, may or may not do what I say and may wait for you to call again because you are just a salesperson selling me.

**What you say:** "Of course, when would be a better time to call?"

**What you mean:** I will call you back and will call you repeatedly until you talk to me.

**Why this happens:** People are busy. Some handle interruptions better than others. Those people who are confident and in control of their situations manage interruptions politely, calmly and with certainty even to the point where they can tell you when to call back, or they will ask for your number and tell you when they will call you back. Those people who are not, don't. This is an excellent tell-tale sign of who you are dealing with.

**Is this a good sign that you will make a sale?** No.

**What you do:** Prepare for challenging work. This will require careful chasing and deft management of how and when you call back. In most cases give it twenty-four hours and then begin again as if you had not called the first time. Twenty-four hours is more than enough time to let the dust settle and Buyer should be clear of whatever distraction was preventing taking your first call.

**Boss?** No. See if you can navigate this situation yourself. If Buyer is the type of person who does call back, Buyer will tell you what the next steps are. If Buyer does not call you back, make a note in the file, find another Buyer in that organization, or move on to another organization altogether.

## The Situation: Following Up

**Buyer Says:** "I have a lot on my calendar right now."

**Buyer means:** I am overwhelmed and work in an overloaded environment.

**What you say:** "That's a great situation! At least you are busy. Please tell me about your development cycle and how would be the best way to get on the calendar in the first place? How do you decide when to take on a new worthwhile product?"

**What you mean:** Everybody is busy otherwise they would be unemployed. That is a poor excuse to put me off. How does one project get assigned priority and the other does not?

**Why this happens:** People do not want to be bothered with more to do when they feel unappreciated or overworked.

**Is this a good sign that you will make a sale?** No.

**What you do:** You must get a slot on the calendar for them to "pencil you in". The first thing is to find out how to be considered for a sale before you are evaluated for a sale. There should be a process for evaluation. Find out what that process is, and then execute against it.

**Boss?** No. This is calendar juggling. Deal with it.

# 3

# Getting the Meeting

**Buyer says:**

1) "We can meet, but it's early in our development cycle, let me get back to you on when would be a good time in a few months."
2) "We have an open-door policy here and happy to meet with you, but I have to warn you this may not be for us."
3) "Let me circle the wagons and then we'll set a meeting."
4) "I don't think a meeting is needed/indicated/worthwhile at this time."
5) "I think meetings are a waste of time. What do we need to discuss?"
6) "It's your dime. When do you want to meet?"
7) "We looked at it, and if we are interested, we will contact you."
8) "You know, this has some merit. I'd like our outside media agency to sit in. When do you want to meet?"
9) "I have my schedule right here. How is next…at…?"
10) "I would like to get more background on your product and what you have in mind exactly. Can you provide more details, and we can discuss a meeting later?"

© Results Through Focus, LLC 2023
A. Berg, *Sales on the Go*, Business Guides on the Go,
https://doi.org/10.1007/978-1-0716-3211-6_3

**Preparing for Getting the Meeting – Three things you need to have before you start:**

1) Know where the meeting is going to be. There is nothing more embarrassing than to ask where. It is ok to confirm the location when you send the meeting invitation, but you should at least know the city/town/state, especially if there are multiple buildings which many large corporations have.
2) Know if you must include Boss either in person, on the phone, or a video call – or Boss's surrogate or representative. That way you can say "we can meet you," or if you are going solo "I can meet you." Don't change the line-up. If you are not sure, default is "we," not "I." It is easier to delete a person (makes you look more important), than adding a person.
3) How do they like to be presented to: Hard copy? Projector? Laptop? It is okay to ask, and Buyer will appreciate your attention to detail.

## The Situation: Getting the Meeting

**Buyer:** "We can meet, but it's early in our development cycle, let me get back to you as to when would be a good time in a few months."

**Buyer means:** I will never call you back. I work in a bloated bureaucracy, or a company run by a megalomaniac control freak, or a company that has trouble making decisions, or we are so regimented by circumstance that anything out of the ordinary is starved to death due to lack of attention.

**What you say:** "That's great you see a meeting as a next step. Regardless of where this fits in your cycle wouldn't it be better to move to the next now, rather than later?"

**What you mean:** Your internal problems are your own, and while I respect them, I need to force the issue, gently. Also, I am actively selling this. By the time you get back to me, the opportunity you see now, but can't act on, may be gone.

**Why this happens:** People are afraid to raise new concepts or situations to associates.

**Is this a good sign that you will make a sale?** No.

**What you do**: If you don't set the meeting now, you never will. If you put the concept of a meeting off, you will never get it. You must keep the conversation on the level of the meeting is going to happen soon. Buyer's next step is to select meeting participants, a date, and location. This is the data you will follow-up with to get. If you can't get to that level in this conversation, move on to the next Buyer.

**Boss?** No. You have a weak Buyer here. Set the meeting if you can, but do not count on a sale.

## The Situation: Getting the Meeting

**Buyer:** "We have an open-door policy here and happy to meet with you, but I have to warn you this may not be for us."

**Buyer means:** I have an open mind and welcome ideas, but either I have reviewed your product and do not see how we will buy it, or you can come in here and change my thinking.

**What you say:** "That is kind of you. I will take you up on your invitation. When is a good time to meet?"

**What you mean:** I can overcome all objections and obstacles. I believe in my product. I believe in myself. I take you to be a fair and honest person who welcomes new ideas.

**Why this happens:** There are people who genuinely enjoy the free interaction of commerce, ideas, individuals, and new opportunities. Seeing how Buyer is not travelling anywhere to have this meeting with you all it will cost Buyer is at most an hour.

**Is this a good sign that you will make a sale?** Yes.

**What you do**: Carpe Diem. You have a willing Buyer who will buy if you can sell.

**Boss?** Yes. Review this situation in detail with Boss and have Boss marshal resources Boss feels you need to close. Give Boss latitude to do so, sit back, and watch Boss earn his salary. Do not complain if you are relegated to the back bench. Boss will help you close this one.

## The Situation: Getting the Meeting

**Buyer:** "Let me circle the wagons and then we'll set a meeting."

**Buyer means:** You may have found me and while I have not hung up on you, I will not discourage you or encourage you by myself. I need to have the opinions of others who are able to help me save my job.

**What you say:** "Super. Let's set a date now and you can confer with your colleagues, but at least we have a date in the corporate calendar, and I can make travel plans."

**What you mean:** I know you really don't have to take much time to "circle the wagons." Seeing how you did not say "no" to the product, let's just set a date, you can "circle the wagons" all you want, and if the opinion of the group is negative you can cancel the meeting.

**Why this happens:** Your Buyer is a classic consensus builder. Buyer needs the company of others to bolster Buyer's position.

**Is this a good sign that you will make a sale?** No.

**What you do:** Get your meeting anyway and as fast as you can. Make it impossible for Buyer to cancel. You need to get into the center of the "circled wagons" to find a new ally because the Buyer is not a strong person in Buyer's organization. If Buyer is forced to decide, Buyer will fold on the side of "no." This is a toxic situation and you do not have much time. Act immediately and move forward aggressively. You are dead in the water if you don't; it's just a matter of time.

**Boss?** Yes. You have the situation under control, but you need play-by-play tactical guidance from Boss to get to either the center of the circled wagons or help identifying a new Buyer when the original Buyer folds or sells you out.

## The Situation: Getting the Meeting

**Buyer:** "I don't think a meeting is needed/indicated/worthwhile at this time."

**Buyer means:** This is a stupid idea. Your product may be smart, but a meeting is stupid.

**What you say:** "I understand you are terribly busy. Would there be a better time to meet, or better way to present this to your company?"

**What you mean:** You have not told me the product either has, or has no, merit. Therefore, I have not heard "no" and until I hear "no" I won't pretend that I have heard "no" no matter how badly you want me to play this game.

**Why this happens:** Sometimes people who are very direct have no idea what they are talking about. This can also be a form of lazy thinking.

**Is this a good sign that you will make a sale?** Yes

**What you do:** Make Buyer comment on the product. Acknowledge Buyer is a busy person but that does not mean the product is not a good product for Buyer. Ask when a meeting is indicated/worthwhile/needed and on what criterion is this judged. Ask to apply those criteria against your product, submit your findings in writing, follow-up and ask for a meeting. If you can meet the meeting criteria, you have a good chance at a sale.

**Boss?** Yes. But Boss will let you run for daylight with this situation. However, to have room to run with the next situation you have to close this sale.

## The Situation: Getting the Meeting

**Buyer:** "I think meetings are a waste of time. What do we need to discuss?"

**Buyer means:** I have seen and heard just about everything and anything under the Sun. Nothing is new to me. I can evaluate what you have to sell without having to endure sifting through whatever salesperson sorcery you are going to cloud my mind with.

**What you say:** "I understand your point of view, but there any number of details we could work out economically during a meeting. These details will surface with or without a meeting provided you are interested in the product. In the long run it will save you time."

**What you mean:** I will subject you to my Salesperson sorcery; it's what I am paid to do.

**Why this happens:** Not meeting with a salesperson is an ego boost to someone who distrusts the sales equation and salespeople, are not a personable people to start with, think they know everything and are poor managers of their time even though they don't think so. The comment is directed to put you in your place; as a poor salesperson doing a bad job with an inferior product.

**Is this a good sign that you will make a sale?** Yes

**What you do**: At least Buyer wants to at talk about the product. That is a good starting point to complete the sale. The meeting has nothing to do with the merits of the product; Buyer is just insulting you to see how you react. Turn the situation around by emphasizing a meeting will save Buyer time and money and you are happy to be insulted if it will result in a sale.

**Boss?** No. Just keep working all the angles.

## The Situation: Getting the Meeting

**Buyer:** "It's your dime. When do you want to meet?"

**Buyer means:** Who am I to say "no" to a meeting? I love meetings, they get me to the end of the day.

**What you say:** "Excellent. What day and time works best for you?"

**What you mean:** I will help you get to the end of another one of your boring days – five in all during the work week - which gets you to another payday and no one has caught on that you are just a cog in the wheel I have to turn and another rung on the ladder I have to climb in your organization to make the sale.

**Why this happens:** Cogs in the machine go round and round. Use this meeting to get to a bigger cog.

**Is this a good sign that you will make a sale?** No.

**What you do**: Make sure you are not meeting alone, otherwise it is a waste of your time. Invite Buyer to include superiors to the meeting and confirm that they are attending before you leave the office to attend the meeting. If superiors cancel, you cancel because your contact does not have the juice to move the sale forward alone. Besides, you need to meet other people to induce positive momentum to what you are bringing to their organization in the event Buyer waffles on the next commitment, which Buyer is sure to do.

**Boss?** Yes. You must tell Boss you are setting a meeting that you may have to cancel if Buyer's bosses do not participate. Keep Boss up to date and advise as matters evolve.

## The Situation: Getting the Meeting

**Buyer:** "A meeting is a good idea. I will get back to you with the players and suggested dates."

**Buyer means:** I am listening to you with one ear and like what you have to say, but I am hearing the siren call of corporate caution in the other. Therefore, I will be happy to see if I can muster internal support, and if I can, we can move to the next step.

**What you say:** "I am glad you agree the idea has merit. Who will you get on board and when do you think I will hear back from you?"

**What you mean:** This is going to be a long day.

**Why this happens:** Organizations breed fear. It is rare you will find someone who can push a project along without finding allies.

**Is this a good sign that you will make a sale?** Yes.

**What you do:** Recognize that consensus building is an art in the eyes in the person being sold to, and unavoidable in the eyes of the person doing the selling. Beauty, like sales, is in the eye of the beholder.

**Boss?** No. Buy a mirror.

## The Situation: Getting the Meeting

**Buyer:** "You know, this has value. I'd like our outside media agency to sit in. When do you want to meet?"

**Buyer means:** I want to siphon off your top line concepts and feed it to other people outside my organization who can use it to make me look good.

**What you say:** "There is certainly opportunity here, and you will see it with greater clarity when we meet. However, I don't meet with people outside your organization. It will be more productive if we meet by ourselves."

**What you mean:** I will not meet with your blood-sucking idea vampires.

**Why this happens:** Some companies work closely with outside organizations to scour the earth for good ideas, meet with those outsiders, and then use the ideas themselves. It is cheaper and safer this way These external players can be so good at this they have Buyer bamboozled to the point where everything is turned away. Then they repackage the idea several months later, call it their own and charge a premium for "genius thinking."

**Is this a good sign that you will make a sale?** No.

**What you do**: Under no circumstances meet with external players when you are pitching your product. Make it clear that if you show up for the meeting and they are there, you will leave. Then if that happens, make sure you do, even if had to fly to the meeting from far away.

**Boss?** Yes. You are a mighty warrior.

## The Situation: Getting the Meeting

**Buyer:** "I have my schedule right here. Can you meet next….at….?"

**Buyer means:** Now's your chance! Are you powerful enough to set your own schedule?

**What you say:** "Yes, I can be there, no problem."

**What you mean:** You are my customer, and I am happy to oblige. I will be there when and where you say without hesitation.

**Why this happens:** Sometimes, but rarely, people are extremely interested in what you have to sell right there and then. When this happens move heaven and earth to get to the meeting. Cancel or move everything else. Worry about logistics after you make the commitment. Do not give Buyer a reason to think you were not expecting this precise response. Act as if you hear it a hundred times a day.

**Is this a good sign that you will make a sale?** Yes.

**What you do:** Pack and smile. It's go time.

**Boss?** Yes. Invite Boss to walk into the End Zone with you. You flip the ball to the Official, you let Boss do the dancing.

## The Situation: Getting the Meeting

**Buyer:** "I would like to get more background on your product and what you have in mind exactly. Can you provide more details, and we can discuss a meeting later?"

**Buyer means:** I would like to pick your brain more; put you off; make you work harder; ask impossible questions; can't decide one way or the other; like to waffle; am detail oriented; not a people person and just plain lazy and you have reached the wrong person, so move on.

**What you say:** "It looks like you have reviewed the materials thoroughly to know you need more information. What areas do you need more data for?"

**What you mean:** I am calling your bluff. If you have read the material, you can answer the question. If not, then you have not and we will both know this, and you are a waste of time. If you can answer the question, I am happy to provide more data.

**Why this happens:** People like this are either risk averse and put things off if possible, or are very detail oriented and do in fact need more data.

**Is this a good sign that you will make a sale?** No.

**What you do:** Drill down until you uncover the motivation. If it is a stall tactic, move on. If it is legitimate, service the request, set a follow-up, and ask for the meeting at the next follow-up contact point.

**Boss?** No. At this point you are working in a coal mine with a nail clipper. Have fun.

# 4

# Negotiating

**Buyer says:**

1) "Thank you for coming. Before we begin, I would like you to meet our attorney."
2) "I have to tell you; your prices are higher than your competitors."
3) "I think you guys should pay us to carry your product!"
4) "This point is just something you and I can have an understanding about and doesn't have to be in the contract."
5) "We don't make any money on this product/in this business."
6) "We would like to buy this product, but we need to defer paying you for it."
7) "We would like to buy your product; what do you think is fair?"
8) "We would like to buy your product; where would you like to start?"
9) "We have put together a proposal; let us know what you think."
10) "We have firm policy guidelines as to how we work and what we will pay for products such as yours."

© Results Through Focus, LLC 2023
A. Berg, *Sales on the Go*, Business Guides on the Go,
https://doi.org/10.1007/978-1-0716-3211-6_4

**Preparing for Negotiating – Three things you need to have before you start:**

1) Know exactly what terms you will and will not accept. Write down your acceptable, and unacceptable terms, review them prior to the negotiation so you are familiar with them to the point where you do not have to refer to notes when speaking, or being spoken to.
2) Use this mantra silently as you negotiate: "Never need what you want, and never want what you need."
3) Remember this famous saying said about house guests: "No company is better than bad company" and paraphrase it for sales: "No deal is better than a bad deal."

# The Situation: Negotiating

**Buyer:** "Thank you for coming. Before we begin, I would like you to meet our attorney."

**Buyer means:** I am determined to take the high ground right from the start, put you on the defensive, make you think about what you are going to say and intimidate you.

**What you say:** "Nice to meet you. However, I did not bring my attorney and therefore cannot continue with the meeting. What would you like to do?"

**What you mean:** Either the attorney goes, or I go.

**Why this happens:** A standard negotiating ploy is to produce an attorney when none is called for. Attorneys can add an air of finality and gravitas that hampers the free flow of negotiations and lends an advantage of surprise to the side bringing the attorney.

**Is this a good sign that you will make a sale?** No.

**What you do:** Either the attorney goes, or you go, but under no circumstances give in. If the attorney leaves, then the Buyer wants the deal more than Buyer wants to intimidate you. If Buyer insists the attorney should stay, then you never had a deal in the first place. The negotiation never goes well for you when Buyer's attorney is present. Be sure

Boss knows your position on this issue in case you must leave the meeting and fly home.

Never talk to an attorney that does not work for you.

**Boss?** Inform Boss of your "no attorney rule" in general discussions during planning meetings you may have. Then, if this situation arises, stick to the policy. You cannot win if Buyer's attorney is present and yours is not, or, you are alone with Buyer and Buyer's attorney.

## The Situation: Negotiating

**Buyer:** "I have to tell you; your prices are higher than your competitors."

**Buyer means:** I know more than you do about your territory. I will not pay more than what I am paying for similar products. Throw your pricing model out the window when you talk to me.

**What you say:** "Of course they do; but then they know the value of their products better than anyone."

**What you mean:** I don't care.

**Why this happens:** This is a standard opening gambit. It is old school and not effective. You are dealing with someone with little imagination or creative thought.

**Is this a good sign that you will make a sale?** Yes.

**What you do:** Plow through the ploy. Dispense with pricing discussions unless and until you re-introduce the Three Vs of Selling:

a) The Vision Proposition – what the world looks like with your product in their company.

b) The Virtue Proposition – what product attributes are unique to your product that make the Vision Proposition so attractive.

c) The Value Proposition – why buying the product is not only cost effective but bestows benefits on a long-term basis that money can't buy.

**Boss?** No. Just another day in paradise.

## The Situation: Negotiating

**Buyer:** "I think you guys should pay us to carry your product!"

**Buyer means:** I am an aggressive, bad-joke-telling old school huckster who likes to see people squirm and sweat while I pick your brain and then send you packing.

**What you say:** "Then we have nothing to discuss."

**What you mean:** I am prepared to walk right now. Either respect the sales environment in which you are the customer, or I leave.

**Why this happens:** This line about you paying them is meant as a crude joke. Crude it is; joke it is not. Buyer is serious.

**Is this a good sign that you will make a sale?** No.

**What you do:** Wait for the response to your reply, above. Unless Buyer immediately backs off this position, leave. If Buyer was seeing what you are made of, Buyer will see it right there and if Buyer respects it, Buyer will back down, and you can go forward with selling. If Buyer sits and watches you leave, you saved yourself a ton of time.

**Boss?** No. But it is a good "war story" to save for drinks.


## The Situation: Negotiating

**Buyer:** "This point is just something you and I can have an understanding about and doesn't have to be in the contract."

**Buyer means:** I want to have two agreements; one between our companies which is recorded in the contract and one between you and me which is not recorded but which modifies the contract, mostly to my advantage.

**What you say:** "No thanks."

**What you mean:** One deal, one contract. Besides, I like my job and want to keep it.

**Why this happens:** People look for the easy way out. This is one of them.

**Is this a good sign that you will make a sale?** Yes.

**What you do:** Recognize the point in question is important to Buyer. Ask why it should be outside the contract. Listen to the point again and concede a contract point on your side to get Buyer's point on the table officially, and in the contract. It is crucial you understand why this point is so important to Buyer, and then give it to Buyer as best you can.

Never, ever, make a side deal.

**Boss?** Yes. Boss needs to know Buyer is a double-dealing weasel so Boss can record this, and other Salespeople can be apprised of this sleaze-ball.

## The Situation: Negotiating

**Buyer:** "We don't make any money on this product/in this business."

**Buyer means:** I want to convince you that our margins are so low on the product, or in our business that we cannot afford to increase our price to accommodate the cost of your product.

**What you say:** "Then maybe you should drop that product, fire your salespeople, or get out of the business."

**What you mean:** What kind of businessman are you that does not make any money? What are you doing with that product or in that business if it does not make money? What kind of management do you work for, and what game are they playing? I just gave you three solutions you did not think of. Do you really expect me to believe you?

**Why this happens:** This is another common, and poor, opening negotiating gambit. People who use it read it in a book. But not this book.

**Is this a good sign that you will make a sale?** Yes.

**What you do:** Stick to the point about how they market a product or work in business that is not profitable. Either call their bluff or have them show you they really do not make money, which is totally bogus.

**Side note:** People who have money know how to make money, inherit money, or raise money. Stick with them.

**Boss?** No. Don't tell Boss you found a Buyer with no money unless you close the sale. But get the money in the bank first; you never know with this type of Buyer.

## The Situation: Negotiating

**Buyer:** "We would like to buy this product, but we need to defer paying you for it."

**Buyer means:** We would like you to give us your product, so we can try it out and then if we like it, pay for it.

**What you say:** "No."

**What you mean:** No.

**Why this happens:** People use this gambit when they want to impress you with the operating capabilities of their company. Their company will take your product and make money with it but would prefer to pay you later after their return on investment is certain. Deferring payment is not "buying" and agreeing to it is certainly not "selling".

**Is this a good sign that you will make a sale?** Yes.

**What you do:** Remind them they want the product in the first place and the price is fair. All they must do is accelerate their payment schedule. Besides, ask them, do you defer payroll, rent, taxes, or utilities? Why then is your product subject to flexible payment plans? Stick to your position. You have no choice. If you bring a deferred sales proposition to your Boss, you will be fired.

**Boss?** No. See above.


## The Situation: Negotiating

**Buyer:** "We would like to buy your product; what do you think is fair?"

**Buyer means:** Please tell us what the most important aspect of the contractual arrangements is. The first thing you tell us reveals the most essential element. We don't care if it's fair, we want to know what you want most of all.

**What you say:** "I am delighted you want the product. Here is what I think is fair."

**What you mean:** The fact you want the product puts me in a defensive position for the first move. I must acknowledge you want to buy the product and in return I will give you my proposal. That is fair.

**Why this happens:** It is a "go along to get along" world. They want it; your job is to sell it. You cannot always start from the high ground. Take the lead and run with it.

**Is this a good sign that you will make a sale?** Yes.

**What you do**: Give them your proposal, which is a fair one to start with. It is a fair proposal because you are good salesperson.

**Boss?** No. Everything is going about as well as it ever goes in sales. Keep going.


## The Situation: Negotiating

**Buyer:** "We would like to buy your product. Where would you like to start?"

**Buyer means:** We want your product but do not know, or don't pretend to know, what the deal structure looks like. We cannot discuss terms just yet and need guidance as to how best to structure terms that reflect our vision for the product.

**What you say:** "I am happy to help. Based on what I know about your business, here is a general description of the structure you would need to set up to best exploit the product's attributes, virtues and unique characteristics that will make you, and it, a long-term success."

**What you mean:** I am not going to discuss specific terms until you see what you need to do to use the product. Setting up the structure I outlined will cost you money, so pay attention.

**Why this happens:** A person's reach exceeds his grasp; or what's a salesman for? Some people want what they want and don't know how to make use of the object once they obtain it. It happens to all of us, so be kind.

**Is this a good sign that you will make a sale?** Yes.

**What you do**: Give Buyer all the guidance Buyer needs. Buyer is overreaching but does not know it. So again, be kind, it could happen to you someday. Buyer is one step away from discussing financial terms. Therefore, refuse to discuss dollars, percentages, territories, distribution, or other specifics of your business until the structure is set up.

This is a wonderful juncture for you to create a structure in Buyer's company that will insure not only the sale of this product on this day but secure your role as a long-term salesperson for other products. Take your time here, be Buyer's friend and you might make a friend. This is a good Buyer.

**Boss?** No. All part of your job, smile; breathe, repeat.

## The Situation: Negotiating

**Buyer:** "We have put together a proposal; let us know what you think."

**Buyer means:** I am an honest broker. You will receive my best offer and if you accept it there will be no headaches later.

**What you say:** "Thank you. I will review it and get back to you immediately."

**What you mean:** Thank my lucky stars - I finally have an easy day. This makes up for all the heart attacks, sleepless nights, anxiety, and teeth grinding I go through all the time. I will give this my full attention and respect the fact you are acting as an honest broker.

**Why this happens:** There are people who would rather do business than play games. These are good Buyers.

**Is this a good sign that you will make a sale?** Yes.

**What you do:** Assess the offer. Do not look for subterfuge. Close the deal, Buyer's initial offer under these circumstances will not improve much, if any at all.

**Boss?** Yes. You found a "keeper."

## The Situation: Negotiating

**Buyer:** "We have firm policy guidelines as to how we work and what we will pay for products such as yours."

**Buyer means:** Don't ask for anything I won't give and know what that is ahead of time.

**What you say:** "That's great! You may be paying more than what I was going to ask for. Tell me your payment guidance and fee structures for my kind of product and I will take it from there. By all means, please go first!"

**What you mean:** Excuse me; you are not as smart as you think you are. What if I accept your terms? Are you prepared to pay what you tell me you are going to pay?

**Why this happens:** Some people think they are negotiating from strength when they dictate terms up front. The jury is still out on that approach.

**Is this a good sign that you will make a sale?** Yes.

**What you do:** Take Buyer at Buyer's word. Make Buyer go first and stick to it. Buyer will balk and open the conversation so that you present your terms first. Do not rise to this bait. Always circle back to Buyer's first statement. Buyer will become embarrassed that Buyer did not think you would respond the way you did, and Buyer will respect you for it. Buyer may even learn something.

**Boss?** No. This is routine. Besides if Boss thinks this was a lay-up, Boss will give you ten hard/bad/dead leads as penance.

# 5

# Closing

**Buyer says:**

1) "Everything seems to be in order. Let me run this up the flagpole and I will get back to you."
2) "I need to get my CEO/CFO/Board of Directors to sign off on this, and then we are ready to go to contract."
3) "These terms are fine, but I have to make sure my subordinate, who will own this project, is on board."
4) "We are ready to go. Please send me the paperwork."
5) "I thought we were ready to go, but we may have to put the project on hold/on the back burner/push it back. I'm sorry."
6) "We are almost there. I have one more thing to check off and we'll be done."
7) "I have just one more/a few more questions."
8) "There is one thing we don't like/are not sure of/need to change."
9) "Can I have your assurance/guarantee/word this thing will work?"
10) "What are my options if this thing goes south in a year?"

© Results Through Focus, LLC 2023
A. Berg, *Sales on the Go*, Business Guides on the Go,
https://doi.org/10.1007/978-1-0716-3211-6_5

**Preparing for Closing – Three things you need to have before you start:**

1) More time than you know what to do with. When you are in closing mode you have nothing to do but close, nowhere else to go except sit at your desk, or sit in the meeting, and close. Do not look at your watch, your computer clock, or the clock on the wall. When you are closing time stands still.

2) A mind-set that does not multi-task. You must have total focus on Buyer. Do not send or answer texts, send emails, doodle, get coffee (if you wear an operator headset) or take a call from anyone except for your mother – maybe – only if you are rich and can walk away from the job. Don't worry – Mom will understand.

3) Iron discipline not to tolerate interruptions. Do not let anyone in your space, wave them in to sit down, motion with one finger you will be with them in a moment, or wave hello. Master the palm up and out "stop sign." Think of it like a socially correct giant middle finger you give to anyone who does not respect your closing-mode zone.

## The Situation: Closing

**Buyer:** "Everything seems to be in order. Let me run this up the flagpole and I will get back to you."

**Buyer means:** I am satisfied that I can put my neck on the line for the deal I am bringing to my management, and told you I could close on, but I have to find either support that insulates me from potential failure, or a sucker to take the fall. If I can find either of those two, we will have a deal.

**What you say:** "I am delighted you want to get this done based on the terms. Is there a way I can present these terms you and I have agreed on to the people up the flagpole? It would be best if our vision for the product/project was seen as a collaborative effort."

**What you mean:** I don't trust you to get it done and you know you need all the help you can get.

**Why this happens:** There are people who can pull the trigger when they are empowered to, and people who can't. You have met the latter.

**Is this a good sign that you will make a sale?** Yes.

**What you do**: Support your Buyer. Buyer got you this far, Buyer will get you the rest of the way. You can't switch horses now. This is a good Buyer who will need your help from time to time, and there is nothing wrong with that.

**Boss?** Yes. Put Boss on stand-by if you need Boss on a call to buck-up Buyer and imbue Buyer with spine if need be.

## The Situation: Closing

**Buyer:** "I need to get my CEO/CFO/Board of Directors to sign off on this, and then we are ready to go to contract."

**Buyer means:** Relax, pal. I closed on these terms and my CEO/CFO/ BOD approval is a formality. They put me in charge, but we all have stockholders to answer to and this is part of our corporate structure.

**What you say:** "Wonderful."

**What you mean:** I trust you and won't worry. If the deal collapses, you, and I both know you have no juice in your shop and are probably on the way out.

**Why this happens:** Some people actually are in charge. What a concept!

**Is this a good sign that you will make a sale?** Yes.

**What you do**: There is nothing you can do but wait. This is about as good as it gets in the life of a salesperson until you get the signed contract.

**Boss?** No. This is going to close, or it isn't. Nothing Boss can do to help you.

## The Situation: Closing

**Buyer:** "These terms are fine, but I have to make sure my subordinate, who will own this project, is on board."

**Buyer means:** I have one more escape hatch to close. If my serf cannot be successful with this product then I will look bad, therefore it is up to my serf to tell me we can make this work.

**What you say:** "That's great news about the terms. I will work with you and your associate to make sure this is successful. Is there anything I can do now with your associate, so we can wrap this up totally or should I just draw up the final paperwork?"

**What you mean:** You might have told me you manage downwards and let subordinates dictate your decision-making process. I would have engaged them sooner. However, now that I know where the fulcrum of power is in your department, I would like to sell them as hard as I sold, you so that this whole exercise is not a waste of time.

**Why this happens:** People are full of surprises and like to throw curve balls. It is a revealing trait of Buyer you were selling. These kinds of people are not trustworthy. Since when do the subordinates run the boss? What kind of person or what kind of company are you dealing with? Don't people do what they are told?

**Is this a good sign that you will make a sale?** No.

**What you do**: Count on the fact you will have to sell this all over again to the subordinate or another Buyer at another company. If this subordinate agrees to the project, consider yourself lucky. At this stage do all you can to insert yourself in the process of selling the subordinate. If you can't put pressure on primary Buyer by saying that Buyer asking the underling for a blessing of the deal is a mere formality and by indicating you are drawing up the contract lets Buyer know of your displeasure with the last-minute revelation of this ridiculous step.

**Boss?** No. Learn to master the intricacies of the Master/Serf relationship in business.


## The Situation: Closing

**Buyer:** "We are ready to go. Please send me the paperwork."

**Buyer means:** I am in charge, and I have made the decision.

**What you say:** "Outstanding."

**What you mean:** I can't believe it.

**Why this happens:** Some people like to close, get things done, and move on to the next issue/event/challenge/project. These are good people to know who don't take anyone's garbage and are movers and shakers. Keep them close and deal with them often.

**Is this a good sign that you will make a sale?** Yes.

**What you do**: Exactly what Buyer tells you to do, when, where, and how.

**Boss?** No. Learn to recognize good people when you meet them and make them your personal contact. You never know when you are going to need good people.

## The Situation: Closing

**Buyer:** "I thought we were ready to go, but we may have to put the project on hold/on the back burner/push it back. I'm sorry."

**Buyer means:** Something unforeseen has come up at the last minute and derailed the project. I may not be able to go forward and rather that cancel the whole thing; I hand you this weak excuse.

**What you say:** "I understand. What is the circumstance that is causing this, and can we work through it now to keep the project moving forward? We were nearly finished with our negotiations."

**What you mean:** This is a huge surprise, and I am on the hook for this deal.

**Why this happens:** Your Buyer has either overreached Buyer's authority to make the deal, or a powerful force in the organization, or from outside, like a Board of Directors member or a large customer with clout, has suddenly intervened. Buyer did not see this coming.

**Is this a good sign that you will make a sale?** No.

**What you do**: You must isolate the circumstance that has put a wrench in the works. Once you know what that is, you can work to overcome it. Don't worry about re-closing the deal at this point. You must find out what the problem is.

**Boss?** Yes. Get help.

## The Situation: Closing

**Buyer:** "We are almost there. I have one more thing to check-off and we'll be done."

**Buyer means:** I am as anxious to get this done as you are. Please be patient.

**What you say:** "I understand. Is there something else you need me to do?"

**What you mean:** I am supportive of your efforts, but please get this done.
**Why this happens:** This kind of person likes to keep people Buyer is working with in the loop and up to date.
**Is this a good sign that you will make a sale?** Yes.
**What you do:** Leave Buyer alone. Buyer will get it done. This is not a red flag. Stand back and wait for the next call. Buyer knows what Buyer is doing.
**Boss?** No. Close the deal and wrap it up for Boss like a present.

## The Situation: Closing

**Buyer:** "I have just one more/a few more questions."
**Buyer means:** I will test you now by making you crazy. I want to see if you can earn my business by not getting upset, exasperated or impatient with the closing process.
**What you say:** "No problem. What can I answer for you?"
**What you mean:** I know this drill and am happy to make you happy in this regard. There is no such thing as too many questions.
**Why this happens:** People like to play games. Know that, recognize that, and play the game so long as it is feasible.
**Is this a good sign that you will make a sale?** Yes.
**What you do:** Let this gamesmanship from this self-styled gamester roll off your shoulders. But just in case it is legitimate, answer the question as best you can as fast as you can. Position the question from Buyer as indeed the last question and if you answer it successfully, which you will, then you can close the deal.
**Boss?** No. Do not use Boss as a crutch and learn to absorb this games-playing on your own. It will happen repeatedly.

## The Situation: Closing

**Buyer:** "There is one thing we don't like/are not sure of/need to change."
**Buyer means:** I have wrestled every concession out of you I could by showing you all but one of my cards. Now I am playing my last card and you know you must make this concession in order to close.

**What you say:** "What's that?"
**What you mean:** Bring it on. I won't make a bad deal just to make a deal, so this better be good.
**Why this happens:** Two reasons are possible:

1) Buyer is playing the negotiating game when Buyer indicated Buyer had closed, so Buyer is not trustworthy or;
2) Someone on the sidelines, but higher up the food chain, is playing this game, or really does have a concern and desired change in the deal at the last minute.

**Is this a good sign that you will make a sale?** Yes.
**What you do:** You have no choice but the find out what the required change/problem is. Make it clear that you will solve the issue and then move to contract, no questions asked, and no more issues from them.
**Boss?** No. You need to answer the question and solve the problem on your own without hesitation or going to Boss otherwise Buyer will know you have no power. You may not have any power, but Buyer does not need to know that. Answer the question, close the deal, and then tell Boss how you answered the question even if you take a beating.

## The Situation: Closing

**Buyer:** "Can I have your assurance/guarantee/word this thing will work?"
**Buyer means:** I want your final commitment to augment my final commitment to this project, so you have as much at risk as I do.
**What you say:** "You have my guarantee that I believe this is the right product/project for you, but ultimately it is up to you to make it work."
**What you mean:** The nature of the free enterprise system is that it is based on risk. Both of us have taken risks and we must live with it.
**Why this happens:** This is a final stab at extracting a concession that no one can make. Making a guarantee about something which cannot be

guaranteed is very much the pure essence of evil in business. It is best not to do it, or even think about it. If you do, it will consume you forever.

**Is this a good sign that you will make a sale?** Yes.

**What you do**: Stand your ground. Your only moral obligation in sales is to be an honest broker. You are not in the business of making guarantees but bringing people opportunities whose terms and conditions are transparent and fair. What happens after that is a matter of hard work, concentration, dedication, and intelligence, and sometimes luck, but there are no guarantees. Do not make a guarantee you cannot deliver on, and this is one circumstance you cannot.

**Boss?** Yes. Tell Boss you stood your ground and would not be compromised.

## The Situation: Closing

**Buyer:** "What are my options if this thing goes south in a year?"

**Buyer means:** What is my exit strategy? I cannot close until I know I can bail out if I lose my nerve.

**What you say:** "Your options in that regard are the ones we negotiated."

**What you mean:** All the terms are in the deal as we discussed them. There is no exit option unless we put one in the terms.

**Why this happens:** People stick their toe in the water and think they are wet all over.

**Is this a good sign that you will make a sale?** No.

**What you do**: Back way, way up. This deal is not going to close as is. Buyer does not know how to get out, Buyer is telling you Buyer will want to get out if the project/product does not meet expectations. You are going to have to drill back down into the nature of the product/project itself and find out what is making Buyer uncomfortable.

It could be the terms, or it could be something in Buyer's organization, or it could be a new circumstance that has recently become known that is affecting Buyer's ability to take the final step. This is serious. Do not let Buyer brush it off but get Buyer to tell you.

**Boss?** Yes. Get help, lots of help.

# Part II

## The Marketing Section

Enjoy my favorite Marketing story:

Some years ago, I had put together an exceptionally large and complex deal for a client. I am not boasting, but the fact that it was a large and complex deal, and worth significant amounts of money, is germane to the story. The problem was, due to all this complexity, the structure of the deal was bolted together loosely.

While the parts were top notch, what was holding them all together was more luck than genius engineering. Any stress on the deal and it might fall apart. We had to get the deal into the market as fast as we could to make sure it hung together.

While things were in flux, I was flipping out (more than usual) in a staff meeting. The stress was apparent, and I was grasping for straws as to how to keep my deal from imploding.

At one point, the head of the Marketing Department interrupted my rant with the kindest words I have ever heard in my professional life:

"Adam, you've done a great job. We'll take it from here."

The hand-off was accomplished. There was nothing more I could do because as a Salesperson there was nothing more I could do. The Marketing Department was responsible now. They would shoulder the burden and see it through because that was their job. I had done mine. Now it was up to Marketing.

You will work in tandem with, sell to, and sell through, a Marketing Department and work with Marketers to get your deals done. Sometimes Marketer works with you, and sometimes Marketer is working at the customer's Company alongside Buyer. Either way, Marketing has a say in what goes on, and what gets sold.

Learn the language of the Marketing world in the sense of knowing what they are saying and what they are not saying. Their job is to reduce the time in the consumer's mind between seeing the product and buying it. Their job is to eradicate any question, or concern, or hesitancy in the consumer's mind which would prevent the consumer from buying it. Sometimes that perspective gets in the way of your sale, and sometimes not. This section will show you both. Marketers are just people, just like you.

And that Marketer who saved me from a brain explosion? He and I became, and still are, close friends.

A Note on Marketer –

In this section we will be speaking about Marketers who are either on your team, or on the potential customer's team. In each instance this will be specified. There are important differences between the two:

**Your Marketer** – This is someone who works in your organization that you confer with. Selling can be a collaborative effort and when any Marketer gets involved that is the case. At times Your Marketer is helpful, supportive, or skeptical and even possibly a deterrent to moving your deal forward for reasons all their own.

**Their Marketer** – This is someone who works for the potential customer. Buyer may or may not bring Their Marketer into the sales equation, but if they do this is one more person you need to sell. Their Marketer has a different perspective on what you are selling and if their organization needs it. As with Your Marketer, Their Marketer can be helpful, supportive, or skeptical and even possibly a deterrent to moving your deal forward for reasons all their own.

How do you learn to deal with this sales environmental factor? Just sell.

# 6

# Research

**Marketer says:**

1) "You are not going to like the data."
2) "Can you help write the parameters?"
3) "If you can't sell it, I can't market it."
4) "Define the customer."
5) "This is going to be easy."
6) "I've seen this movie before."
7) "This is too complicated to explain."
8) "We looked at two groups."
9) "The results are inconclusive."
10) "How do you want this to go?"

**Preparing for Research – Three things you need to have before you start:**

If you are not already familiar with the rudimentary basics of statistics, then become so. It is hard, but nothing is easy, so suffer. There are primers online and in the library. Do not go into a research situation and not

© Results Through Focus, LLC 2023
A. Berg, *Sales on the Go*, Business Guides on the Go,
https://doi.org/10.1007/978-1-0716-3211-6_6

know what is being said. You do not need to know as much as the statistician, but you need to know enough to ask questions and answer basic questions as well.

Be able to state the names of three research-oriented organizations and/or governmental bodies that are relevant to your business (US Department of Commerce, as an example).

You may be tasked with producing a research model, or comment on one that is presented to you. Know the basics of a research model along the lines as well as you know how to read a balance sheet or an annual report.

If you cannot speak the basics of research, then the researchers will not take you seriously, will not do your work, and will leave you in the dust. Respect them in the same way you want them to respect you. If you do not, they will laugh at you when they go to conferences or do whatever they do for fun.

## The Situation – Research

**Your Marketer:** "You are not going to like the data."

**Your Marketer means:** The assumptions you made going into the sale are not supported by our findings in the Marketing Department. Our findings are more powerful than your assumptions because we have a budget for research and all you have are your instincts. You may have to re-tool your deal or adjust it somehow. You may have industry statistics and all that stuff, but that is old data. We have new data that is proprietary to us and much more accurate, according to us.

**What you say:** "What won't I like about it?"

**What you mean:** Be precise. Be right. Then tell me how this affects the deal I made. It is my option to ignore your data. You cannot impose a new outcome unilaterally.

**Why this happens:** It could be because the deal you sold does not support a long-held concept of, prejudice towards, or consensus for, a desired outcome that is contrary to what the deal you sold, or are proposing to sell, is to the Marketing Department's belief system and by extension, the reason they exist in the first place.

Remember that corporate departmental belief systems are the stuff fiefdoms are made of. Careers and reputations are made on certain overarching declarations as to how the world works. It could be because they are favorite customers of the Marketing Department that the Marketing Department favors because they feel that customer supports the best interests of the Company and your deal challenges that world order.

It could also be because your deal demonstrates that all the money the Marketing Department spent on the data is flawed and someone, somewhere either created a flawed study or did not catch the errors.

**Is this a good sign you will make the sale?** Yes. Your deal will bring in revenue. Their data is spent money. Your job is to open doors and find new revenue. Let someone else tell the Company the Company cannot have the new revenue because the data does not support the outcome – which is – new revenue, thanks to you.

**What you do:** Put the money on the table. Watch the world burn.

**Boss?** No. Boss loves money.

## The Situation – Research

**Your Marketer:** "Can you help write the parameters?"

**Your Marketer means:**

A) I am a total pro and want this project/sale to maximize the opportunity for all involved. Therefore, we are going to combine our expertise – your sale of the project – and my go-to-market – skills to ensure success. OR

B) I am in way over my head and need you to write the business plan for the marketing function I must perform but I can't admit that I need this kind of help.

**What you say:** "Of course!"

**What you mean:** First I need to figure out if you are a competent marketing professional or a marketing amateur who does not know what you are doing. Either way I am going to help you, but what I determine as to your true status will shape my expectations of this exercise.

**Why this happens:** In each case Your Marketer is asking for help. This is acceptable. If Your Marketing person is competent then help that person to your full extent. It will be fun. You will learn something. You will have all sorts of input and be exposed to new ways of thinking and doing things.

If Your Marketing person is not competent, then Your Marketer will be helpful as you help write the parameters. You will shape the marketing portion of your sale in your own image, control the process, gather insights, extend your control without anyone knowing it.

In all fairness to all Marketers there could be situations where, no matter how competent they are, your deal may have bought them to a new frontier of marketing that while general principles apply, specifics as to the area of business you sold in may not be totally clear to the Marketer. This is okay; you don't know everything, either.

Or Your Marketer could use your help. Your Marketer determined that you are a good person who they can ask for help, without having to ask for help. Additionally, if you supply parameters in this instance, you create an unspoken bond that will pay positive dividends for you, Your Marketer and your organization for a long time to come.

**Is this a good sign you will make the sale?** Yes, and make a new friend.

**What you do:** Whatever it takes to set forth the paraments.

**Boss?** No. You can handle this. Your Marketer is your friend and yours alone.

## The Situation – Research

**Your Marketer:** "If you can't sell it, I can't market it."

**Your Marketer means:** I am under pressure from my Boss to get the marketing function in gear for this project you are selling. I am putting you on notice for two things; you need to sell it and if you can't then I don't look bad or if you do sell it, I can market it, but the cart cannot go before the horse, and I have told my Boss as much.

**What you say:** "That makes total sense and I look forward to getting this done and in your hands."

**What you mean:** Game on!

**Why this happens:** Some companies are under so much pressure to get product to market that the onus falls on the Marketing Department to set up for product advancement via advertising and promotion that the sales portion becomes an afterthought. This is especially true when the product is heavy in manufacturing complexities, or regulatory considerations, or demands from retailers that want assurances the Company will support the product, or competitive pressures. Also, salespeople know not to count chickens before they hatch, but at times, marketers are choosing the recipe and lining up the ingredients before chicken is hatched.

Also, this pre-planning is the nature of marketing. Marketing must react to what Management has arranged to have sold, and therefore Marketing wants to get going on projects as soon as possible, even if it means not having the product sold. It is best to get used to this different mindset. It's not bad, just different. And a fact of corporate life. Get used to it, and even better, embrace it and make allies in any Marketing Department.

**Is this a good sign you will make a sale?** Yes. Pressure from Your Marketer will make you a better salesperson.

**What you do:** Go out and make the best sale you have ever made. Take advantage of the fact you have a Marketer who needs to get your sale into the market.

**Boss?** Yes. Boss will want to know where pressure is coming from inside the organization. Your Boss will talk to Your Marketer's Boss and get things squared away. That is what Bosses get paid to do.

## The Situation – Research

**Your Marketer:** "Define the customer."

**Marketer means:** Who did you just sell this to?

**What you say:** "Let's set up a time to go over the customer profile that I put together so you can penetrate the target and develop a robust set of marketing concepts to generate sales."

**What you mean:** I sold it to the person who bought it.

**Why this happens:** Even though you and Your Marketer work for the same Company, the pressures to get things done are different at different stages of the revenue generating process. Marketers want to understand as much as they can about the potential customer for the product you sold so they can allocate resources appropriately and effectively. Hence, the more they know about the customer the easier their job is – which is not a dreadful thing – you want your job to be easier too just from a different perspective. Remember your job is to sell and get the money. Sometimes the person with the money is not the exact target customer and this prompts Your Marketer to ask you to define who you just sold the product to.

Afterall, Your Marketer must parse the marketplace and make the most sense of it. Your Marketer will start with you to point them in the right direction seeing how you bought them this mess.

**Is this a good sign you will make the sale:** No. Even if you have made the sale, if Your Marketer cannot define the customer, Your Marketer is marketing to, and Your Marketer has the clout, Your Marketer may go to Management have you cancel the sale or re-negotiate the sale to better fit a long-term success profile and a more perceived reliable repeat customer.

**What you do:** Rework your notes on the customer into a memo to Your Marketer in a language Your Marketer can understand. However, keep in mind that you cannot always sell to the person who has the money. The sale needs to make sense throughout the process especially when there are multiple and/or powerful stakeholders. If you make this mistake of selling only to the highest bidder when that strategy is not called for, you will make that mistake once. This is what "know your customer" means.

**Boss:** Yes. Tell the Boss you have been asked to define the customer. Boss will understand.

## The Situation – Research

**Their Marketer:** "This is going to be easy."

**Their Marketer means:** Either I am going to have a lot of fun with this project, or I have done this before and know the drill.

**What you say:** "That's the best news I have had in a long time!"

**What you mean:** I can go on to the next sale. Let me know if you need me for something.

**Why this happens:** Sometimes you catch a break. Sometimes Their Marketer catches a break. Nothing is easy. If it was, we would all still be living in the trees eating bugs. But every once in a while, the stars align and it's all downhill even when you did not have to climb to the top of a hill in the first place.

**Is this a good sign you will make the sale?** Yes, as close to certain as certain can be even if the money is not in your bank in the form of salary or commission.

**What you do:** Move on to the next sale without looking like you are abandoning the project. Make sure Their Marketer can contact you at any time, even though you both know Their Marketer won't.

**Boss?** No. Moving on means moving on.

## The Situation – Research

**Their Marketer:** "I've seen this movie before."

**Their Marketer means:** I have bad news for you.

**What you say:** "Did it win an Oscar for Best Sale?"

**What you mean:** I've seen this movie too. It is titled "Sell and Repent."

**Why this happens:** When it is said that Marketing is different than Sales, this is a good case in point. Sometimes a good sale, or a closed sale, results in the creation of a product, or service, which is monumentally hard to pull off, or bring forward to market. It happens sometimes. You sold it, and now you will pay. What looks simple to a Salesperson can be overly complex to a Marketer and vice versa.

In this case Their Marketer has been through a similar situation and is kind enough to let you know there are issues. And not just any issue or issues. Issues Their Marketer has dealt with before to bad outcome. Their Marketer is giving you a heads up.

**Is this a good sign you will make the sale?** No. There are issues. Do not go to the bank yet.

**What you do:** Buckle up.

**Boss?** Yes. Early and often.

## The Situation – Research

**Your Marketer:** "This is too complicated to explain."
**Your Marketer means:** Get out of my way.
**What you say:** "Okay."
**What you mean:** Fair warning taken. I will leave it to you. Contact me when you want to explain further if you want to explain it at all. I'll be in my office or reachable on the road.
**Why this happens:** Marketing can be complex. In many cases it is way more complicated than sales. If your product that you sold is comprised of many elements, then the matrix of marketing disciplines needed, and the coordination of same, can be so intricate that a Marketer does not want to give you a college level course on what the next steps are right there, at that time. Listen to Your Marketer – get out of the way.
Once the project is complete, and the urgency has subsided it is appropriate for you to go back to Your Marketer and ask for a debriefing. Everyone learns from this; you learn the finer details of marketing and Your Marketer has a chance to hone skills explaining what had to happen and why as Your Marketer may need to explain to an audience more important than you.
**Is this a good sign you will make the sale:** Yes. Your Marketer is on board with your sale but just does not have time to bring you into the process of marketing it.
**Boss.** No. If you are going to confess ignorance don't do it when a third party has locked you out of the knowledge loop.

## The Situation – Research

**Your Marketer:** "We looked at two groups."
**Your Marketer means:** We didn't like the results of the first group so we went back and found another group to see if we could juice the data more to our liking.
**What you say:** "And…"

**What you mean:** Just give me the best data. I don't want to know how you got there or what the other group had to say. Do not make me go back to my customer and unravel some aspect of what has been agreed to just because the data is funky.

**Why this happens:** Expectations are hard to square with the world we live in. Theories are not facts. Your sale is a fact; it has happened, and it looks like a conundrum or an unexplained cosmic phenomenon when viewed by Your Marketer. For this fact to fit into a structure conceived to execute certain pre-determined plans nine times out of ten, and then it doesn't, the Marketing Department has to scramble. This scrambling can take the form of interrogating not one, but two, groups of potential customers, to see which marketing approach is best. Then Marketing must choose. And Marketing hates to choose. Marketing must set up a second group, pay for it, explain it, and then justify the choice.

**Is this a good sign you will make the sale?** Yes. It's somebody else's problem.

**What you do:** Offer to understand the data from both groups but do not offer to fix anything with your sale. Let Your Marketer pound the square peg into the round hole. They chose to find alternative data, let them deal with it.

In any case, making sausage is disgusting.

**Boss?** Yes. But just in passing. If the Boss wants to find out more, he will. Stay out of it.

## The Situation – Research

**Their Marketer:** "The results are inconclusive."

**Their Marketer means:** We are unable to make sense of the data.

**What you say:** "How so?"

**What you mean:** What is inconclusive? The data that precipitated in pure form, or your interpretation of the data?

**Why this happens:** Nothing is inconclusive. Inconclusive means there is no apparent or easy decision to make, and it will require more study. There are subtle nuances, tiny spaces in the world that we need to drill down into to find the answer. Imagine a world without microscopes.

If you looked at a puddle of water and your result was inclusive as to whether there was life in that puddle, your results could be wrong. Until you put a drop on a slide under a microscope and look closer. Inconclusive in the world of Sales and the world of Marketing means someone needs to work harder. Or adjust the lens.

**Is this a good sign you will make the sale?** Yes. Someone must work harder. Not you.

**Boss?** No. It will sort itself out.

## The Situation – Research

**Your Marketer:** "How do you want this to go?"

**Your Marketer means:** You have a choice; I can school you now, or school you later.

**What you say:** "I didn't know I had options but thank you."

**What you mean:** "Thank you, I think." You and I both know I am going to learn something new, and it is not going to be fun, or pretty.

**Why this happens:** Do not even attempt to steer or influence events from here on out. You will be eaten alive and then spat out. You in the domain of a seasoned, savvy, experienced, highly competent Marketer who has uncovered events, circumstances and forces you can neither predict, understand nor control.

Ask Your Marketer what your options are. Then ask what Your Marketer recommends. Then do not ask why. Just go along with the recommendation.

When you hear this phrase, it means you are in way over your head and even if you feel you are not, a determination has been made that you are. If you go against this, you will make powerful enemies.

Your Marketer is not asking you to help decide as to what the best direction is. You are going to be told. You are being told you have a choice, but in reality you have no option. I call this "The One Choice Option."

**Is this a good sign you will make the sale?** Yes. If you go along.

**What you do:** Do what you are told. Ask no questions.

**Boss?** No. Absolutely not. Your Marketer has already discussed this with your Boss, and they are watching to see what you do. Shut up. Go home.

# 7

# Strategy

**Marketer says:**

1) "This is a high-level analysis."
2) "Here is the view from thirty thousand feet."
3) "Our strategy is anchored…"
4) "Our strategy is informed…"
5) "We are starting from the ground up."
6) "We are going to start from the top down."
7) "This is how we do it."
8) "Our strategy has always been…"
9) "The data suggests we use this/a new/approach."
10) "Here is what we are going to do."

**Preparing for Strategy – Three things you need to have before you start:**

Strategy is one of the most used, uttered, spoken, written, quoted and ubiquitous words in the business world. In no other area of life do you hear it spoken as often as one does in the pursuit of profit. You don't hear

© Results Through Focus, LLC 2023
A. Berg, *Sales on the Go*, Business Guides on the Go,
https://doi.org/10.1007/978-1-0716-3211-6_7

other people who are earning a living use the word "strategy" to describe what they do as often as people in business settings do.

Therefore, do not use it unless:


A) You can define it in one sentence and
B) You mean to use it.


Here is my definition of strategy: An actionable dynamic purposed to achieve a desired result in a specified circumstance.

I only use "strategy' when I have conceived of, or are prepared to conceive of, an actionable dynamic to achieve a desired result in a specified circumstance I will take responsibility for seeing through.

## The Situation – Strategy

**Your Marketer:** "This is a high-level analysis."

**Your Marketer means:** We expect you to buy-in to our findings.

**What you say:** "Well, let's look at the methodology and the conclusions."

**What you mean:** I am open to the data and am not going to come to a judgement just now, or, because you tell me to.

**Why this happens:** When there is a lot at stake, a "high-level" analysis puts everyone in the process at stake. The "stakes" depend on who you are and where your interests reside.

No matter where your position is in the Company be aware of the stakes and sensitivities around that. It can be a mine field if you are aggressive or pigheaded. It can be a boon to your career if you can demonstrate to the stake holders that you are on board, even if you are not initially.

Do all you can to integrate the "high-level" analysis into your replies and then your subsequent actions. A regular analysis is not a "low-level" analysis, but a regular analysis gives you a greater degree of latitude if you want to challenge the methodology and/or the conclusions.

If you are asked to comment on a "high-level" analysis, and you are not totally in agreement, keep that to yourself. The best thing to do is to ask a question about the methodology. It is easier for Your Marketer to explain how they got there, as opposed to what they found when they got there.

**Is this a good sign you will make the sale?** Yes. Don't make a scene.

**What you do:** Embrace the "high level" analysis for what it is and be happy Your Marketer put the resources against the project.

**Boss?** No. Boss is happy Your Marketer did not ask him for any money for the analysis.

## The Situation – Strategy

**Your Marketer:** "Here is the view from thirty thousand feet."

**Your Marketer means:** I am a new and expensive hire with friends in the C-Suite. I have no idea what I am doing or what this about, but I have to say something. So, I will offer a perspective that anyone can have by looking down at the Earth from thirty thousand feet and telling you if it is day or night.

**What you say:** "It will be very helpful if we can get a broad view on this situation."

**What you mean:** Must be nice to fly first class on somebody's else's dime.

**Why this happens:** Friends like to hire friends.

**What you do:** Enjoy your seat in coach.

**Is this a good sign you will make the sale?** Yes. Just smile and nod.

**Boss?** No. You don't know who the Boss's friends are.

## The Situation – Strategy

**Your Marketer:** "Our strategy is anchored…"

**Your Marketer means:** I know what anchored means.

**What you say:** "A strong anchor is needed in order for salespeople to go out and know what they do has foundational support. Thank you. Please go on."

**What you mean:** I can go along with this. Makes sense to me. Now that we have established that you know what anchored means, let's see if you know how to lower it and then raise it so we can move to a new position when needed. So far, so good.

**Why this happens:** Reference to an anchor is not a bad thing. In this case it means that Your Marketer is a fundamentalist in the sense that elements of a plan have to be ordered and logical. Nothing wrong with that in a world full of chaos.

A reference to an anchor may not be an indicator of a revolutionary approach, or game changing attitude, but it can be especially useful for you, the Salesperson, in that it brings you back to basics and focuses your thinking on what can be accomplished without thinking up a new Theory of Relativity, which is always exhausting.

Embrace the pedestrian. No one ever got a speeding ticket walking.

**Is this a good sign you will make the sale?** Yes. Your Marketer is happy to have your sale.

**What you do:** Learn the words to the United States Navy hymn "Anchors Aweigh." You probably don't know it, so don't pretend that you do, so look it up.

**Boss?** No. Just another good day.


## The Situation – Strategy

**Their Marketer:** "Our strategy is informed…"
**Their Marketer means:** I know current buzz words.
**What you say:** "I am happy to curate this situation with you."
**What you mean:** I know current buzz words, too!
**Why this happens:** Buzz words are just curse words but with good PR.

People curse because they cannot command standard language in a situation that does not rely on shock value. When people curse it is not necessarily when a person is under stress. Sometimes people sprinkle curse words into normal conversation for emphasis or to ensure attention. Think of cursing as a form of passive aggressive bullying using speech instead of physical or emotional assault.

Now, replace cursing with buzz words. Buzz words are meant to be exclusionary. If the other person is not up on their current buzz words, they are left out of the conversation. If a person is shocked or offended by curse words, they are left out of the conversation because they do not want to be part of the conversation or cannot participate on the same level because they choose not to curse.

It is the same with buzz words; you are left out of the "club." The implication socially is that you are not "cool." The implication professionally is you are not up to date reading relevant industry publications. This implication can be false. You may be up to date, just not wired to rely on buzz words as a crutch to hide incompetency.

In both cases - use of curses or buzz words - the non-participating person is at a distinct disadvantage.

**Is this a good sign you will make the sale?** No. You are being tested by "the Cool Kids".

**What you do:** Make up your own buzz word right there, on the spot. Then watch the reaction. A buzz word wizard will not admit they do not know a buzz word and will not challenge you. Then you are on even ground. Fight for your sale.

**Boss?** No. Boss knows all the buzz words that ever were, or ever will be.

## The Situation – Strategy

**Your Marketer:** "We are starting from the ground up."
**Your Marketer means:** If I had my way you would all be fired.
**What you say:** "Let's get started!"
**What you mean:** It's going to be a long day.
**Why this happens:** Your Marketer may have a point. Just be sure Your Marketer is not referring to you. In fact, this could be a good sign if you are not the target. You can be a true asset for Your Marketer in helping to start from the ground up. You can have important impact to shape future outcomes if you buy into the original premise that something, somewhere needs to be re-created from the ground up.

This can be a lot of work, and hence a long day, or series of long days, but can be well worth it.

However, to be on the safe side in your internal dialogue, be sure Your Marketer is just not saying things that need to be re-built from the ground up because Your Marketer has no other thoughts.

**Is this a good sign you will make the sale?** Yes.

**What you do:** If you are not told what your role is going to be in this effort, ask, and accept the answer, and then get to work on it. Visibly.

**Boss?** Yes. Tell Boss where ground is being broken. He will hand you a shovel.

## The Situation – Strategy

**Their Marketer:** "We are going to start from the top down."

**Their Marketer means:** I love to make minute adjustments and make them look like brilliant strokes of genius.

**What you say:** "I know where we can have early and positive impact if you want my input."

**What you mean:** If this makes you happy it makes me happy. Nobody ever tweaked themselves into a massive world-ending disaster and took everybody with them.

**Why this happens:** This approach is indicative of a failure of imagination. Their Marketer is attracted to, taken by, or bewildered with, bright shiny objects. All sorts of analogies apply; they love to season the gravy rather than figure out how to cook the meat, they love to ice the cake rather than mix the batter, they love to countersink the nails than cut the boards, etc.

Adjusting the obvious is easy to see and can be mistaken for true work, especially in a fast-paced and loosely disciplined organization. Bright shiny objects also can have bells and whistles and blinking lights, so, by focusing on the small things, some people, especially incompetent or uncaring executives, can be fooled.

**Is this a good sign you will make the sale?** Yes. Nothing bad is going to happen so long as the window dressing does not crack the glass.

**What you do:** Nothing.

**Boss?** No. Boss is not fooled.

## The Situation – Strategy

**Your Marketer:** "This is how we do it."
**Your Marketer means:** No strategy needed.
**What you say:** "I heard about your approach; very interesting."
**What you mean:** You had your fifteen minutes of fame and I heard about it. I'm not going to tell you what I heard, or what I think, just that I heard about it. You are famous, but I will let you figure out why.
**Why this happens:** People get set in their ways yet manage to find themselves in positions where flexibility and adaptability are key skills needed to succeed and help their team succeed.

However, many organizations promote and encourage rigidity as a counterbalance to free-thinkers and disrupters. In this case, you have run into a strait-laced linear thinker who brings this kind of approach to bear or has been told to do so. In any event, there is no way around it.
**Is this a good sign you will make the sale?** Yes. Your sale is part of the already established order of how things are right now. Don't change anything.
**What you do:** Listen politely and see where you fit in. You will fit in somewhere, otherwise you will not be part of the process.
**Boss?** No. Boss knows "how we do it."

## The Situation – Strategy

**Their Marketer:** "Our strategy has always been…"
**Their Marketer means:** Our strategy is not so much a strategy but a method, and I do not know the difference. However, if I had to express what we need to do as a "strategy" then I would have to set out "tactics" to follow the "strategy" and while I don't know what a "strategy" is, I know what "tactics" are, and I am too lazy to create those. Thus, I rely on methods, not strategy.
**What you say:** "If the strategy has worked before, it will work now. Let's see what we need to do."

**What you mean:** I am always the team player and will go along with calling a method a strategy. Maybe I will learn something in the work we do. Besides, I am not going to call you out on this because I do not want to get in my own way and possibly cost myself a sale.

**Why this happens:** There can be legitimate reasons why a certain project, task or sale does not need a strategy. At times, the task at hand is simple enough to warrant an applied method and no strategy is needed.

Why Their Marketer may have to state that the work ahead of the team is based on a "strategy" rather than a time-tested method is Their Marketer may be under pressure from Management to re-tool the method as a "strategy" to justify the staffing or expense involved.

Furthermore, strategies are not always static directions to get things done. Strategies evolve. Strategies also can be set ways of doing things, such as in chess. However, no chess player would tell you that a specific move of one piece to one square on the board is a "strategy."

Look at it this way: There are strategies to clean an entire house, but cleaning methods to clean hardwood floors are different from methods for cleaning windows. Both of which are part of the strategy to clean the house.

**Is this a good sign you will make the sale?** Yes.

**What you do:** Go along for the ride. Learn something new. Make sure your sale is airtight.

**Boss?** No.

## The Situation – Strategy

**Your Marketer:** "The data suggests we use this/a new/approach."

**Your Marketer means:** We have a situation on our hands, and we are going to have to figure this out.

**What you say:** "Let's start with the data, and then what do you suggest?"

**What you mean:** Lead, and I will follow.

**Why this happens:** Your Marketer knows what they are talking about, knows exactly what needs to be done, and is a natural leader. Hitch your wagon to this person and go where you are taken. This will be an excellent experience all by itself, and so will anything else Your Marketer gets involved with.

**Is this a good sign you will make the sale?** No. If your sale does not measure up, it will be in trouble. If you lose this deal, it will be for an exceptionally good reason. Learn from it and don't resent a negative outcome or you will never be on Your Marketer's team again.

**What you do:** What you are told.

**Boss?** No. Boss knows who the good people are. If you mess this up, Boss will know, and you will get a talking to for certain.

## The Situation – Strategy

**Their Marketer:** "Here is what we are going to do."

**Their Marketer means:** I have looked at the situation, gotten the assets together, and developed a plan that I believe will work. Who is with me?

**What you say:** "Good."

**What you mean:** I don't have to think anymore, just do. I could use that kind of break.

**Why this happens:** Their Marketer has seen this movie before, knows what needs to be done, by whom, and in what order. Their Marketer can see the outcome; it is only a question of how long it is going to take to get there. Their Marketer also does not waste time or suffer fools and gets right to the point. Their Marketer is someone to hitch your wagon to and get involved in anything this person is working on.

**Is this a good sign you will make the sale?** Yes. Your sale has been factored in and found worthy.

**What you do:** Accept your place in the plan. If you are asked to pitch in with something additional, do so with a smile on your face.

**Boss?** No. Boss is glad you are busy.

# 8

# Planning

**Marketer says:**

1) "We scheduled a Brainstorming Session."
2) "I'm forming a task force."
3) "Where do you see yourself in this project?"
4) "Who do you want on your team?"
5) "What do you think of so-and-so for such-and-such?"
6) "We are purpose driven."
7) "What are our competitors doing?"
8) "Please submit your plans to me within X business days."
9) "What are the odds of this happening?"
10) "What is your Plan B?"

**Preparing for Planning– Three things you need to have before you start:**

1) Be more open than usual to new ideas – everyone is going to have something to say.
2) Do not chomp at the bit, many people have different senses of urgency.
3) Simpler is better. You can always add details later.

© Results Through Focus, LLC 2023
A. Berg, *Sales on the Go*, Business Guides on the Go,
https://doi.org/10.1007/978-1-0716-3211-6_8

Impress people with your clarity of vision, concise thinking, and economy with words. Do not be viewed as a waste of time by wasting other people's time.


## The Situation – Planning

**Your Marketer:** "We scheduled a Brainstorming Session."
**Your Marketer means:** I am out of ideas.
**What you say:** "I am basically free for the next few days. Let me know when."
**What you mean:** I'll go along with this waste of time. Let me find my Thinking Cap.
**Why this happens:** This is another foray into the land of buzzwords and time sinks. Whenever you hear "Brainstorm" you are sure to have the meeting start with two other tired entreaties: "Put your Thinking Caps on" and "There are no bad ideas." Then, the poor sap that has to run the meeting will stand in front of a white board or large sheets of paper and wield a felt tipped marker. Next the question/problem/issue/will be presented and solutions asked for. A couple of moderately good ideas will be proffered but in about five minutes all the people in the room who think they are funny, but are not, will pipe up with rude or cliché "jokes" and forced laughter will ensue. This will last two hours. Snacks and coffee will be served. Then it will end.
Take aways:

> A) There is no such thing as a Thinking Cap beyond the third grade.
> B) There are bad ideas. Lots of them.
> C) Everyone thinks they are a comedian. Professional comedians know better.
> D) This is a politically important waste of time that you must enthusiastically participate in.
> E) The extroverts in the group always dominate. Their "thinking" prevails. The introverts are left out and so is their "thinking." Therefore, the results are suspect because the sample is skewed.

F) There is nothing wrong with getting a group of people together to discuss ideas. Just call it that: a group of people meeting to discuss ideas.

**Is this a good sign you will make the sale?** Yes. Brainstorming has nothing to do with selling, or your sale.

**What you do:** Hang in there. Under no circumstances make a joke but laugh at the jokes others make.

**Boss?** No. Notice no Boss goes to Brainstorming Sessions. Ever.

## The Situation – Planning

**Your Marketer:** "I'm forming a task force."

**Your Marketer means:** I am leaping before I look.

**What you say:** "All hands on deck!"

**What you mean:** I guess the Brainstorming Session was a total failure.

**Why this happens:** Louder speaks action than words. Yes, that's right. "Louder speaks action than words" means histrionics and chaos will now take the place of hard work, attention to detail and well-reasoned progress towards a logical and attainable goal.

When Your Marketer declares a task force is going to be formed, then the next step which will take weeks if not months is to enlist or draft (depending on the clout Your Marketer wields), the people on the task force.

The people on the task force may or may not be the right people. That is another consideration. The task force could a crack team of focused commandos who can get the job done right the first time, or a clown car jam packed with ne'er-do-wells, hangers-on, glad-handers, grifters, jerks, bottom feeders, leaches, morons, con-artists, parasites and goof balls who will suck up the budget and write a report that masks the total incompetence of Your Marketer.

A "task force" is a committee with money to burn.

**Is this a good sign you will make the sale?** No. The task force will crush your deal if it does not fit the pre-determined outcome. It does not matter if there are effective or ineffective people on the task force because everything is in play.

**What you do:** Document why your deal needs to survive. Lunch will be served. So, eat; it may be your last meal for a while.

**Boss?** Yes. Get to the Boss immediately with your documentation and have Boss get you off the task force and protect your deal. This is a Boss 911. Bring Boss a sandwich.


## The Situation – Planning

**Your Marketer:** "Where do you see yourself in this project?"

**Your Marketer means:** I don't want you on this project.

**What you say:** "I think the best place for me is where you think I can contribute the most."

**What you mean:** I go where I'm wanted.

**Why this happens:** You have made the sale and there is no more room on this project for you. Your Marketer wants to name the team, and you are not on the team. The reasons will never be made clear to you.

You did your job, move on, and such is a life in Sales. Sometimes you are not the star even if you bring in the money. If this is the case, do not take it very seriously. You cannot be on every team. You will get your commission.

In some cases, Your Marketer may have a point, so do not be too judgmental. Your Marketer may feel there is a distinct dividing line between Sales and Marketing. Also, Your Marketer may feel that you are better off spending your time making another sale.

Your Marketer is usually right. This is a gift.

**Is this a good sign you will make the sale:** Yes. Being on the team has nothing to do with the sale.

**What you do:** Go on to the next sale.

**Boss?** Yes. Boss knows this happens because Your Marketer would not have excluded you without checking with Boss. Just confer with Boss so he knows you know, you are okay, and off to the next sale. Be a warrior.

# The Situation – Planning

**Your Marketer:** "Who do you want on your team?"
**Your Marketer means:** You are on the team.
**What you say:** "Wow! That is great! I would like X to be on my team."
**What you mean:** I am going to put your best friend/closest ally/person you want to spy on me on my team. I know who that is, but you do not know that I know that. That person will feed you only great things about me because I am going to engineer the situation to do exactly that.
**Why this happens:** Your Marketer may want you on the team because you have the insider knowledge about the deal you sold to maximize collective results. This is good! You are viewed as an asset. This also happens because Your Marketer may want to learn how you do things. This is also good! If you prove your value in a marketing setting you will be on a lot of Your Marketer's projects.
As to your selection of team members, you want to name people Your Marketer wants on the team, not who you want on your team. Use this opportunity to bond with people you would not otherwise bond with under normal sales-only circumstances.
Choose who Your Marketer wants, and you will be friends forever. Name your own friends, and you will not be on Your Marketer's team again.
Look at it this way; You get to name the team and be the Team Manager. Concentrate on the task at hand and burnish your image as a rainmaker who can inspire others. This is a huge win for you.
**Is this a good sign you will make the sale?** Yes.
**What you do:** Name the team. Then host a team lunch (pizza in the conference room is fine) No afterwork event; no alcohol.
**Boss?** No. You know the right people to put on your team. If you don't, then yes, ask Boss.

# The Situation – Planning

**Your Marketer:** "What do you think of so-and-so for such-and-such?"
**Your Marketer means:** This is a loyalty test.

**What you say:** "They could be a great choice for this project."
**What you mean:** I know a mine field when I step in one.
**Why this happens:**
This question is set up to see if you understand Your Marketer's need to have you conform to Your Marketer's expectations as to how the world should be ordered. Therefore, there is no right answer. There is no right combination of people in the organization for any project that will satisfy Your Marketer. So, don't even try.

The operative word in your answer in this specific case is "could." "Could" is a qualified agreement. There "could" be circumstances that work against your named candidate that you can always point to that mitigated the best outcome.

You cannot be right. State your answer with the "could" word and see where the conversation goes.

**Is this a good sign you will make the sale?** Yes. Your Marketer does not care about the sale. Scuttling the sale only makes more work for Your Marketer and gets Boss involved. This is about the game, not the money.

**What you do:** Accept the dictated outcome. Don't start a fight you cannot win.

**Boss?** No. There is nothing anyone can do.

## The Situation – Planning

**Their Marketer:** "We are purpose driven."
**Their Marketer means:** I do not tolerate debate or dissent.
**What you say:** "Excellent. We can get things done!"
**What you mean:** Don't look to me for any meaningful input.
**Why this happens:** The "Purpose Driven executive" replaced the "Hard Charging executive" several years ago when "Hard Charging" as a descriptor became associated with bullying and harassment and consequently lawsuits. Corporate buzzword gurus and slang masters initiated the change to divert focus away from an older way of treating people in organizations and towards a dedication to profit and "shareholder value."

Who can argue with that?

What you are left with as the Salesperson is a hard charging executive in purpose driven clothing. Do not be fooled. This kind of person, whether they are in Marketing or not, is not prone to fair minded evaluation of what you think. They do not care. They want things done their way.

The "purpose" will be clear because it will be stated to you. It is also clear who will do the "driving."

**Is this a good sign you will make the sale:** Yes. Again, the sale has nothing to do with Their Marketer's perception of reality or place in the pecking order.

**What you do:** Go about your business on this project as you are instructed.

**Boss?** No.


## The Situation – Planning

**Your Marketer:** "What are our competitors doing?"

**Your Marketer means:** Whether we are proactive or reactive, we need to understand what is happening around us.

**What you say:** "I can give you a top line right now, and then follow-up with a more detailed analysis."

**What you mean:** I get it, and I have valuable information.

**Why this happens:** Your Marketer is not afraid to ask for marketplace intelligence from any source to help advance the project. This is a great development because Your Marketer is not a know-it-all, not a control-freak and is not afraid to admit not knowing everything. It takes strength and courage to admit this kind of thing in an organization and this should be applauded.

Not only should it be applauded but you should weld yourself to Your Marketer just for these reasons. Also, you need to provide timely, accurate and insightful marketplace intelligence. Not only will this show you know your territory, business, accounts, and clients, it will allow you to demonstrate your unique insightful and penetrating analytical abilities. It will round you out and make you more valuable than you already are by virtue of your sales acumen.

To people who are not in sales, a salesperson who can sell is one thing; a salesperson that can sell, and think, is quite another.

**Is this a good sign you will make the sale?** Yes. Your sale is folded into the project and even if the marketplace intelligence is not good news. Your Marketer will find a way to counter-market or ramp up competitive assets.

**What you do:** Write up your analysis. Be right.

**Boss?** No. Not right now. Share the marketplace intelligence findings when the report is complete.

## The Situation – Planning

**Your Marketer:** "Please submit your plans to me within X business days."

**Your Marketer means:** I have a job to do and a limited time to do it. I need everyone to adhere to the schedule.

**What you say:** "No problem."

**What you mean:** I will drop everything to get this done by the deadline.

**Why this happens:** Nothing wrong with having a deadline. It keeps things organized, disciplined, and moving forward. This Marketer is not only schedule-centric but detailed oriented. This is not a waste of time, nor should it be a burden.

There is no such thing as an unreasonable deadline if the deadline serves to advance profitability and success of the project. Even if other factors come into play, such as a business trip, if Your Marketer has sway over your career, it is best to cleave to the deadline, take a deep breath, get a cup of coffee, and prepare for overtime.

**Is this a good sign you will make the sale?** Yes. Just cooperate with Your Marketer.

**What you do:** Do not tell Your Marketer you will provide the plan prior to the deadline. Your Marketer has heard this before. Action speaks louder than words, and this is all Your Marketer cares about, and rightly so.

Hand in the plan at least twenty-four hours prior to deadline. Will you be sucking-up if you do? Yes, but do not be concerned what others think about that. Nobody that counts, cares.

**Boss?** No. Boss expects you to beat the deadline by at least twenty-four hours.

## The Situation – Planning

**Your Marketer:** "What are the odds of this happening?"

**Your Marketer means:** I have no back-up plan and rely on intangibles for certainty.

**What you say:** "Fifty-fifty"

**What you mean:** I cannot help you if that is all you have.

**Why this happens:** Clearly Your Marketer does not understand the sales process. There are no odds to quote because there are so many factors at play in a sale that nothing is ever certain except a fully executed contract and money in your bank account.

However, there are people in this world who grasp for, and cling to, belief systems that falsely permit a degree of comfort when no such comfort should be offered. Rather than look for odds, Your Marketer should ask: "What can we do together to close this sale so I can get on with my marketing function?" This question prioritizes assets and time to maximize effort against a target.

However, that question will not be asked because that would require marketing pre-work. By asking for odds Your Marketer can place blame on you if your quote low odds and the sale does not get made or take credit for the sale if the odds are high.

By saying "fifty-fifty" you are indicating you will not play this game. You work in a business, not a casino.

**Is this a good sign you will make the sale:** Yes. Your Marketer is just looking for something that does not exist in the world of sales; certainty.

**What you do:** Work to get the deal done, like with any other deal.

**Boss?** Yes. Boss likes to know who the odds makers are. And Boss likes a good laugh, too.

## The Situation – Planning

**Their Marketer:** "What is your Plan B?"

**Their Marketer means:** I am not expecting your Plan A to fail, but it is best to have a back-up plan. Please tell me what it is.

**What you say:** "Glad you asked. Plan B is…"

**What you mean:** I am not expecting Plan A to fail either, and always plan ahead.

**Why this happens:** Their Marketer is asking a sound, reasonable question. In no way should you interpret this question as some sort of failure or shortcoming on Their Marketer's part. Their Marketer is looking out for you, your sale, your Plan A and also whatever departments or associates are attached to the project or sale. Their Marketer is covering all the angles, all the bets, and works on contingencies.

**Is this a good sign you will make the sale?** Yes. If Plan A bombs, the sale can close based on Plan B.

**What you do:** Always have a Plan B worked out. This is a good Marketer. For extra points make sure Plan B is as good as Plan A. This is twice the work but well worth it. Keep Their Marketer close to you, you will learn a lot and make money in the process.

**Boss?** No. Boss expects you to have a Plan B.

# 9

## Tactics

**Marketer says:**

1) "Let's get as much free publicity as we can."
2) "We have to be aggressive."
3) "Where do you want to start?"
4) "This packaging is not going to win any awards."
5) "Make it go viral."
6) "We need a force multiplier."
7) "Our campaign should speak for itself."
8) "Let's talk metrics."
9) "We have to tap into trends."
10) "The timeline is critical."

**Preparing for Tactics– Three things you need to have before you start:**

1) Understand the difference between strategy and tactics and be able to speak to this in one short sentence because someone is bound to ask you at some point.

© Results Through Focus, LLC 2023
A. Berg, *Sales on the Go*, Business Guides on the Go,
https://doi.org/10.1007/978-1-0716-3211-6_9

2) Be able to give an example of how you used tactics, not strategy, to close a sale. My definition of a tactic: An action in support of achieving a goal or objective.
3) While strategy relies on planning, tactics relies on logistics. Understand your supply chain, the supply chain of your customer, the day-to-day resources you will need to execute the tactics, and where the weak points are and where the strengths are in the distribution networks.

## The Situation – Tactics

**Your Marketer**: "Let's get as much free publicity as we can."
**Your Marketer means:** I believe there is such a thing as a free lunch.
**What you say:** "We'll squeeze out as much as we can, but do we have a budget just in case?"
**What you mean:** There is no such thing as a free lunch.
**Why this happens:** In many cases the pressures on the Company to adhere to a budget set by the Company's bankers and/or owners is so intense that it strangles any creative breath out of the Marketing, Sales and Product Development departments can muster individually or collectively.
This pressure affects executives in varying degrees and in this case Your Marketer has succumbed. Thus, the order goes out to find what can be "purchased for free", which is, as it was meant to be, an oxymoron.
In all cases, if it is free, it is not worth the effort and does not return much in the investment, seeing how there is no investment.
Also in all cases, everyone says you have to spend money to make money, just some spend more than others.
**Is this is a good sign you will make the sale:** Yes. The sale is not in jeopardy. The effort and resources to support the business the sale has initiated, is.
**What you do:** Just go about your business. However, look for work slowly and silently. It is not a good sign for the Company in general if Your Marketer has been reduced to finding free publicity akin to posting flyers on the bulletin board near the cash registers in the local supermarket.
**Boss?** No. Prove you are plucky by volunteering to distribute flyers.

## The Situation – Tactics

**Their Marketer:** "We have to be aggressive."

**Their Marketer means:** I am not good with nuance, modulation, or patience when it comes to slackers, but I have to make a blanket statement.

**What you say:** "I'll leave no stone unturned."

**What you mean:** I don't leave any stone unturned as a matter of course as I do my job, but nobody is going to accuse me of being a wimp by not agreeing with your mindset.

**Why this happens:** In all fairness to Their Marketer, Their Marketer may be setting a tone for the team. There may be people on the team who do not have a "bias for action" (a favorite buzz phrase of people who by nature are not biased to action but heard it someplace, and like a suit of armor made of aluminum foil, find it looks better than it works.) and Their Marketer has to set an attitudinal orientation for the less bias action inclined.

So, go with that for now. Their Marketer is not pointing to you, but pointing over your head, like when you were in school, to the jerks sitting in the back of the room.

**Is this a good sign you will make the sale:** Yes. Their attitude has nothing to do with your sale.

**What you do:** Send in an aggressively worked report from time to time.

**Boss:** No. This is all part of your day in Sales.

## The Situation – Tactics

**Your Marketer:** "Where do you want to start?"

**Your Marketer means:** Why am I asking you?

**What you say:** "Let's start with the customer's budget."

**What you mean:** Why are you asking me? I must give you an intelligent answer and cannot be flippant. By starting with my customer's budget, I can work with information I control and give you some purchase to craft a plan that will not embarrass anyone.

**Why this happens:** People run out of ideas, or don't have ideas, or don't know what ideas are, or repeat what was last told to them. Clearly Your Marketer does not know the first rule of leadership; the Leader always has a Plan, even when the Leader does not have a Plan. Any declarative statement (See – "We have to be aggressive") cannot be construed as a plan.

A plan does not have to be good; it doesn't even have to work; it just needs to be a set of sequential action steps (more than two action steps to be precise) to be defined as a Plan.

When you are asked "where do you want to start" this is a complete abrogation of responsibility to concieve of a Plan, and is indicative to what is to come. What is to come is worse than chaos. What is coming is entropy.

**Is this a good sign you will make the sale?** No. Everything is in danger. Chaos you can deal with, entropy, where all systems fall apart, you cannot.

**What you do:** Cobble something together and hope for the best. Do this from the safety of your newly constructed bunker.

**Boss?** Yes. But you do not need help. Tell the Boss you started with the customer's budget in case Your Marketer tells Boss you were asked where you wanted to start.

## The Situation – Tactics

**Their Marketer:** "This packaging is not going to win any awards."

**Their Marketer means:** The money is in the bank. I am burnishing my resume. I wish I had been in Graphic Design.

**What you say:** "We should track sales and go from there."

**What you mean:** Good product will overcome bad packaging, but good packaging will not overcome bad product.

**Why this happens:** Let the sales record stand on its own. It is interesting that the advertising industry has awards for great packaging but there is no corresponding body of award recognition for the product that sells the most. That is because packaging is subjective, and sales is not.

Furthermore, the bestselling product is most likely something immune to packaging influence such as telephone poles or wheat or sand.

Their Marketer has come to the packaging process way too late. The process was delegated, and the result is not to satisfaction. However, clearly it was to somebody's satisfaction within budgetary and time constraints or it would not have gotten to the stage where it could be critiqued.

Their Marketer has declared an opinion, is going to book the money the product generates regardless and put the Graphics Department on notice to do better next time even though next time Their Marketer is still not going to get in front of the packaging process at the concept stage.

**Is this a good sign you will make the sale?** Yes. If Their Marketer is not going to kill the sale based on an opinion about the packaging, the sale is not in jeopardy.

**What you do:** Listen attentively to what is wrong with the packaging, pretend to make notes, say thank you, and go back to work.

**Boss?** No. Nothing to see here, move along.

## The Situation – Tactics

**Your Marketer:** "Make it go viral."

**Your Marketer means:** I love the Internet and have no idea how it works!

**What you say:** "I'll post it to Social Media."

**What you mean:** Like you know what Social Media is. Now leave me alone.

**Why this happens:** "Going viral" did for marketing on the Internet what tonic water did for gin: made it palatable, but nobody knows why.

Going viral is a sales myth. It may have currency in some quarters but like lightning, it is so powerful it cannot be stored. If it has gone viral then you will know about it after the fact, and never before. "Going viral" is a line you know you have crossed when you see it in the rear-view mirror.

"Going viral" is as impossible to predict as it is to manufacturer. Do not pay attention to Your Marketer in this instance.

**Is this a good sign you will make the sale?** Yes. The emphasis on "Going Viral" is post-sale wishful thinking.

**What you do:** Make sure the search history on the Company server is flooded with entries for "Search Engine Optimization" and SEO. Make it look like you are searching for how to find the unicorn.

**Boss?** Yes, but over drinks. A good war story for your book.

## The Situation – Tactics

**Their Marketer:** "We need a force multiplier."

**Their Marketer means:** I, and hence we, do not have what we need to make this work.

**What you mean:** "I can talk to X."

**What you mean:** What do you do all day? Stop playing video games and get back to work.

**Why this happens:** If you are in Sales for a living, chances are you were not the kind of student that handed in homework late. Therefore, being part of a conversation where you are asked to find a "force multiplier" is foreign to you.

Seeking a "force multiplier" in a business situation, let alone a Marketing situation, means you live life way behind the eight ball and let things happen to you.

Part of effective marketing is to identify, qualify, align, and deploy the assets you have to support the sale. Stating you need a "force multiplier" means you have no force to start with. And you are right there in the middle of this mess.

It also means you are counting on a lot of luck to jump start a moribund communications effort.

**Is this a good sign you will make the sale?** Yes. The Sale is the force. The trick is to find the multiplier.

**What you do:** Make some calls and see if you can enlist an ally. Be helpful.

**Boss?** No. This is part of your job.

## The Situation – Tactics

**Their Marketer:** "Our campaign should speak for itself."

**Their Marketer means:** I rest on my laurels.

**What you say:** "The product can do most of the talking if that is what you mean."

**What you mean:** You are not making any sense. If the campaign does not have a message, then how can it speak for itself?

**Why this happens:** Their Marketer has a long track record of success. It is a good bet that some of the campaigns Their Marketer has worked on or been largely responsible for are based on pithy, easy to understand, easier to remember one or two words or a very memorable short phrase. You can't argue with success.

But you can argue with using past success to replace effort, imagination, and hard work. This phrase practically orders people to come up with a sure-fire winner that will change the face of marketing. Not that Their Marketer will have anything to do with that effort except to claim the credit.

And you were right in the first place; it makes no sense.

**Is this a good sign you will make the sale?** Yes. Their Marketer is so not about your sale.

**What you do:** Pitch a non-sequitur as a catch phrase for the campaign. Their Marketer will love it.

**Boss?** No. Again, just another day at work dealing with people.

## The Situation – Tactics

**Your Marketer:** "Let's talk metrics."

**Your Marketer means:** The data will drive the process. We can make great things happen when we understand the world we are working in.

**What you say:** "I have preliminary data right here and get you whatever you need right away."

**What you mean:** Somebody gets it.

**Why this happens:** There are people in this world who are task focused and results oriented. They do not have pretenses or live in a fantasy or a dream. They begin and end with data. Data determines strategy, tactics, and next steps. Your Marketer is a good person, knows "what is what," and how to get things done. Your Marketer may wind up running the world, so stay close to this person.

It does not get better, or simpler, than this.

**Is this a good sign you will make the sale?** Yes. The sale is the end all and the be all. It is where the data resides.

**What you do:** Sharpen your pencil, open the calculator app on your phone and update the business applications on your computer.

**Boss:** No. Happy day.

## The Situation – Tactics

**Their Marketer:** "We have to tap into trends."

**Their Marketer means:** We are not cool.

**What you say:** "Let me check with a few retailers."

**What you mean:** We do not tap into trends; trends tap into us.

**Why this happens:** If you have to tap into a trend, then the trend is over. Seeking to tap into a trend is like being a surfer surfing the back of a wave. Sure, it will lift you, but you will not be propelled forward and absolutely no one can see you.

When you are ordered to tap into a trend you can be certain that the thinking around your project is stale, and shop worn. It may even have been taken out of long-term storage. That means people, or the person, responsible for marketing your project are not committed to it or think poorly of it or have something better to work on.

When it comes to trends, trends have to find you in order to be part of it. Ultimately, the trend chooses you, not the other way around.

**Is this a good sign you will make the sale?** Yes. If there is no sale, then there is nothing for the trend to tap to.

**What you do:** Check with your retailers and write a clever memo on what you found out from them.

**Boss?** No. Don't let on that someone thinks your project is not cool.

# The Situation – Tactics

**Your Marketer:** "The timeline is critical."
**Your Marketer means:** We need to execute well, and precisely.
**What you say:** "We should constantly review where we are in the process."
**What you mean:** I agree.
**Why this happens:** Your Marketer knows what is happening, and why, and understands how important time and timing is to get the project done and maximize positive results.

Anyone who can use time as a tool to good purpose has a firm handle on reality. Perhaps they suffer a reputation for cracking the whip or being a task master, but that kind of criticism is usually unfair and comes from people who do not have a good sense of time or urgency.

In many cases, timing is crucial, deadlines must be met. The train leaves the station when the schedule says so. Your Marketer knows the trains run on time.

**Is this a good sign you will make the sale?** Yes. You have an ally when it comes to a healthy respect for time.
**What you do:** Execute the plan according to Your Marketer's direction. Keep this person close. They know what they are talking about.
**Boss?** No. Boss knows time is money.

# 10

## Return on Investment

**Marketer says:**

1) "It's hard to assess what role that factor played."
2) "Some things surfaced we did not expect."
3) "Please write an after-action analysis."
4) "Let me bring you up to speed."
5) "The project has a lot of topspin on it."
6) "We need to double down."
7) "When it gets granular, we'll see a different picture."
8) "We have more work to do."
9) "The results are in."
10) "The model needs some work."

**Preparing for ROI– Three things you need to have before you start:**

1) Enlist someone in the Accounting Department to keep you briefed on what may happen, so you are not surprised by events.
2) Memorize the Company mission statement and vision so you can quote it if need be.
3) Have a back-up forecast so you can obtain a do-over if the ROI is low.

© Results Through Focus, LLC 2023
A. Berg, *Sales on the Go*, Business Guides on the Go,
https://doi.org/10.1007/978-1-0716-3211-6_10

There is nothing like friends in high places, and the Accounting Department is the highest place in any Corporation because that is where decision makers go to make decisions. Cultivate real friends there, understand what they do day-to-day and comply with everything they ask for, when they ask for it, without hesitation or interpretation. Get them whatever they ask you for immediately. They will help you out when you need help especially when the ROI is not on your side.

Quoting the Company mission statement and vision means you are on-board and a team player.

Prepare a back-up forecast in case your first forecast is rejected, but don't tell anyone you have it. If you need it, you can produce it the next day. If you do present it the next day, tell everyone you worked all night on it. Practice looking like you did not sleep that night.

## The Situation – Return on Investment

**Your Marketer:** "It's hard to assess what impact your work had on getting the project finished."

**Your Marketer means:** I'm cutting you out of any credit you might have been entitled to for getting this project off the ground.

**What you say:** "I don't understand. Could you put that in an email to me so I can review the situation?"

**What you mean:** I know exactly what you are trying to do, and I am going to make you put it in writing for the record, for everyone to see.

**Why this happens:** Greed. Pure and simple, greed. Greed to protect revenue; greed to deny commission, greed to deny or take credit, greed to award recognition to someone else. Malignant greed – just for the joy of it. Greed – because Your Marketer can.

**Is this a good sign you will make the sale?** No.

**What you do:** First, come to grips to the fact that you may lose this sale and there is nothing you can do about it. However, this is not your default position on the matter. Get the explanation in writing if you can. If you cannot, then feign surprise, failure to understand and indignation until it gets attention.

Also, life is not fair. Welcome to Sales.

**Boss?** Yes. Boss needs to know who is hurting Boss's team member. Boss will understand that you are not the last, and you are not the first. If Your Marketer is immensely powerful, Boss may be next.

## The Situation – Return on Investment

**Your Marketer:** "Some things surfaced we did not expect."
**Your Marketer means:** We need you to revise the deal you closed.
**What you say:** "Well, that happens sometimes. What do we need to think about?
**What you mean:** I need to know how heavy a lift this is going to be.
**Why this happens:** This happens and do not be surprised. This may, or not may not be, bad. Not all adjustments are made equal, and some deals are easier to unwind than others. You have been asked to renegotiate a deal and depending on the status of the paperwork you may or may not be able to. You are obligated to examine what can be done, but you do not have to do it if it puts you in a bad situation professionally. Circumstances vary, but this request from Your Marketer does not.
**Is this a good sign you will make the sale?** Yes. The original deal will hold together. If you cannot renegotiate, chances are Your Marketer will go with the original terms, but Your Marketer is under pressure to accommodate the wrinkle and will put undue pressure on you to fix the situation.
**What you do:** Under no circumstances compromise your integrity. If push comes to shove, have Your Marketer make the call to your customer. Look at what can and cannot be done. This is a good juncture to understand why sales and selling is about relationship building. You need relationships to find out what is possible.
**Boss?** Yes. Ask Boss to involve Legal to provide cover and make sure you are not doing anything wrong.

## The Situation – Return on Investment

**Your Marketer:** "Please write an after-action analysis."

**Your Marketer means:** Something went wrong, and I am not going to tell you what it was, but I need to know what you know so I can best frame my report to Management.

**What you say:** "Sure! When do you need it?"

**What you mean:** Not my problem.

**Why this happens:** You've heard the expression: "The Devil is in the details." This is an example of that. If the details are not thought out, or glossed over, they come back with a vengeance. Somewhere something seemingly small was left out or overlooked and now it has surfaced in a big way.

When you are asked to author a report about what happened, as opposed to a report, or plan, about what will happen, you can be sure something did not go according to plan - a plan you had nothing to do with. Your Marketer is not going to tell you everything that went wrong because Your Marketer has to limit the fallout.

However, because your sale, and your deal, sits at the center of the issue Your Marketer is struggling with, you have been asked to write a history. You must comply. This is not an unreasonable request and will be helpful to Your Marketer.

**Is this a good sign you will make the sale?** Yes. Your sale is water under the bridge. The problem now is the bridge has collapsed.

**What you do:** Write the after-action analysis as best you can and keep Your Marketer a friend. As far as you know you did not make the mistake so draft the report in a neutral voice.

**Boss?** No. Do not trouble Boss's tranquil state of mind.


## The Situation – Return on Investment

**Their Marketer:** "Let me bring you up to speed."

**Their Marketer means:** The project is well on its way to success!

**What you say:** "Wonderful. What's been going on?"

**What you mean:** I'm going to learn something now.

**Why this happens:** This is a good Marketer. Their Marketer wants to fill you in on the details to round out your sales experience and give you some pointers on what to look for next time you make a sale on something Their Marketer is involved in. Nothing wrong with that. You will learn something. Keep in mind Their Marketer is taking time out of the day to give you these details.

**Is this a sign you will make the sale?** Yes. This is not about the sale.

**What you do:** Nothing. There is nothing nefarious in this so don't look for anything nefarious. Take a deep breath and enjoy the lesson.

**Boss?** No. Nothing could be simpler.


## The Situation – Return on Investment

**Your Marketer:** "The project has a lot of topspin on it."

**Your Marketer means:** It is totally out of control.

**What you say:** "That project is a great opportunity for a lot of people."

**What you mean:** Should I duck, run, or shelter in place?

**Why this happens:** In another day and age, a project that has gotten out of control would have been chalked up to the "law of unintended consequences." Because in today's day and age nobody can admit to anything being "unintended" nor face "consequences" the term "topspin" has been seconded from tennis to capture the feeling of helplessness when corporate types watch a project explode on impact, crash, and burn, or maul a group of innocent bystanders.

Alternatively, it could be that the project succeed beyond wildest expectations and bust the budget because there is more money coming in than was planned for. This can be bad too because it means budgeting was inaccurate and forecasting was off target.

Anything that has "topspin" is not planned for, and that all by itself is a disaster even if it makes buckets of cash.

This happens because marketplace intelligence is flawed. The flaw can be anything and there are too many factors to list as to what exactly is flawed. It could also be due to flawed methodologies, assumptions, and the theory of the case. These are the three main culprits.

**Is this a sign you will make the sale:** Yes. Upending this sale would just make things worse.

**What you do:** If the consequences are bad look around like you have no idea what is going on. If the consequences are good, count your money.

In both cases if you are involved in planning make sure your market-place intelligence is accurate, your action steps are based on past demonstrable outcomes and your methodologies are sound.

**Boss?** No. A train wreck is a train wreck.


## The Situation – Return on Investment

**Their Marketer:** "We need to double down."

**Their Marketer means:** The project is not working, and the product is not selling.

**What you say:** "How so?"

**What you mean:** I am not going to double down on anything until I know what is happening and why.

**Why this happens:** There are situations where the sale you made does not work out. The contract is signed, the product, whatever it is, is not meeting expectations. The initial efforts Their Marketer has made by plan to support your sale is not enough.

If could be a bad product. It could be a weak customer. You may have made sale that was not well thought out. Market conditions may have changed to the adverse. It could the marketing message was not well conceived or executed. It could be a lot of things. That is not the point. The point is the money is not coming in and you have been asked to help.

This not Their Marketer's fault. You could be at fault. Or nobody could be at fault. It could just one of those things.

**Is this a sign you will make the sale?** Yes. But you may wish you had not.

**What you do:** Figure out where the problem is. If it is a sales related issue you can impact, then do so. If the problem is in another department, offer to help.

**Boss:** No. Boss sees the numbers. If Boss wants to talk to you, Boss knows where to find you.

## The Situation – Return on Investment

**Their Marketer:** "When it gets granular, we'll see a different picture."
**Their Marketer means:** If I examine things more closely maybe the outcome will change.
**What you say:** "I'm happy to wait, if you think that will help."
**What you mean:** The sum of the parts, no matter how small the parts, will never be greater than the whole. You can try all you want, but nothing is going to change.
**Why this happens:** People who cannot see the larger picture for whatever reason tend to look for data that will change the outcome in tiny packets. As the aggregate data continues to fail their expectations, they look for smaller and smaller data packets in the misguided hope that there is a better answer on an atomic scale.
**Is this a sign you will make the sale:** Yes. But be prepared to be part of the drilling down process to help Their Marketer examine whatever is considered granular.
**What you do:** Have as little as possible to do with this exercise. It makes you look like a nitpicking small-minded loser. Let somebody else provide you with the granular data and then do your analysis. If you get involved with this process, you will always be asked to be part of it.
**Boss?** No. Boss likes the big picture but always knows that getting things done means tending to details, but not granular details.

## The Situation – Return on Investment

**Your Marketer:** "We have more work to do."
**Your Marketer means:** Saddle up.
**What you say:** "Got it".
**What you mean:** Let me get my horse.
**Why this happens:** Despite best efforts from intelligent people things do not go as well as we would like. Despite best efforts from intelligent people things go better than planned. Either way, there is work to be

done either to mitigate a problem or to press an advantage when new opportunities arise due to hard work and good product.

Your Marketer can recognize both outcomes. This is particularly good and takes a good Marketer to act in either case.

Your Marketer has analyzed the data and determined that you, the salesperson on the project should be tapped to do more work.

**Is this a good sign you will make the sale?** Yes. You will maximize the outcome by fixing the issue or creating new opportunities.

**What you do:** Whatever Your Marketer asks you to do. Your Marketer has the information to deal with the situation and you need to do the work. There is nothing wrong with work.

**Boss:** No. Don't look to discuss a problem you are working to fix, or take early credit for a better situation that may evolve.

## The Situation – Return on Investment

**Their Marketer:** "The results are in."
**Their Marketer means:** Surprise!
**What you say:** "Surprise me!"
**What you mean:** You are a sadist.
**Why this happens:** People like to keep information to themselves so they can leverage you. This happens in personal situations too. It is a form of control, however, not all forms of control are malevolent.

In this case, when you hear the phrase "the results are in," it really means that Their Marketer has had the opportunity to review the results in private, and then package how Their Marketer tells others about the results so it reflects best on Their Marketer, and no one else.

When results are organized that means there is a quiet and thoughtful mind at work.

**Is this a good sign you will make the sale?** Yes. The sale was never in doubt. What the surprise is, is another story altogether.

**What you do:** Hold your breath.
**Boss?** No. Boss does not like surprises, good or bad.

## The Situation – Return on Investment

**Your Marketer:** "The model needs some work."

**Your Marketer means:** Things did not go well on this project. I am giving you cover by blaming the model.

**What you say:** "That's a surprise. We were working according to a plan. How can I help you fix it?"

**What you mean:** Thank you, thank you, thank you.

**Why this happens:** Your Marketer is a good person. Your Marketer will take the heat and sees a flaw in the model, or the plan, or the algorithm – whatever – and will blame that instead of a human, specifically you. Your Marketer likes you. Don't ask why.

**Is this a good sign you will make the sale?** No.

**What you do:** Accept the fact that the model is flawed and therefore the deal is contaminated and should be trashed. If it goes forward, so much the better, but do not count on it. To save you, Your Marketer must sacrifice the sale.

Do not complain. Indicate you understand without saying as much. Count Your Marketer as fair person and do Your Marketer a favor in return as soon as you can.

**Boss?** No. Boss is already aware of a flawed model. No need to dwell on it.

# Part III

## The Management Section

Corporate, top-level Management and Corporate, top-level Sales are always in dynamic tension. This situation filters down to all levels of Management and Sales including the level where it is just your Manager and you as Sales. The degree of tension varies, but it is always there and always in flux, which is why it is called "dynamic tension." When you are dealing with Manager and Management, at any level, be aware of this and be sensitive to the amount of dynamic tension you are exposed to in any situation.

The reason for this is because as a Salesperson, and working in Sales, you are an agent of change. You upset the equilibrium in any system. The system you have upset then works to achieve a new equilibrium. The cycle repeats itself. If you sell and push the system, the system will push back against you, regardless of how much money you make for the system. Do not confuse Management with the system. Management always wants money, but the system wants peace and quiet at any cost.

That is why when a Salesperson, or any agent of change in a closed system, encounters Management things tend to slow down. Sometimes slow down a lot, sometimes a little, and sometimes but not often, not at all.

The point is Management is reviewing, examining, and contemplating what is poking the system.

You, the Salesperson, are doing the poking, and the Manager responds. You will sell to Managers inside and outside your organization. They are just like anyone else, just like Buyer and Marketer and Boss.

Everyone has a job to do, and no matter what you hear, or how what you hear is portrayed in this Section, Manager is doing what Manager is paid to do.

It's not all bad. In many cases Manager will save you from yourself and when they do you may not even be aware of it.

Give them a break.

# 11

## Explain

**Manager says:**

1) "Got a minute?"
2) "Let me show you this."
3) "Have you ever heard of/do you know?"
4) "Part of what we do around here is…"
5) "I read your report."
6) "This comes from the top…"
7) "We've reached a consensus."
8) "One of our Board members…"
9) "I am of the opinion."
10) "Let me stop you there."

**Preparing for Explain – Three things you need to have before you start:**

1) Drink some herbal tea and relax.
2) Always know your top three accomplishments without looking at notes and be prepared to speak to them calmly.
3) Practice nodding in agreement.

© Results Through Focus, LLC 2023
A. Berg, *Sales on the Go*, Business Guides on the Go,
https://doi.org/10.1007/978-1-0716-3211-6_11

Be prepared to listen to Manager. It may be good, it may be bad, but you must listen.

Keep in mind the Salesman's Mantra: "The simple truth is, the truth is always simple."

## The Situation – Explain

**Manager:** "Got a minute?"
**Manager means:** This is important to you.
**What you say:** "Of course."
**What you mean:** I am ready for anything.
**Why this happens:** Impactful news is best delivered succinctly. News, any news good or bad, delivered in a corporate environment is best delivered, as far as Management is concerned, as a surprise because Management does not like leaks.

When the Manager uses the phrase "Got a minute?" it is a catchall for something that is going to affect you one way or the other but is personal to you. Could be a promotion and a raise, it could be termination. When you hear it, something is about to happen.

This is a precision surgical strike, for better or worse.

**Is this a good sign you will make the sale.** If it is good news, yes. If it is bad news, no.
**What you do:** Rise to the occasion, whatever it may be, and be the pro that you are. Smile, look Manager in the eye, shake hands and say: "Thank you."
**Boss?** No. Boss was informed way before you were.

## The Situation – Explain

**Manager:** "Let me show you this."
**Manager means:** Something has happened that involves you, that we have to talk about, and which you are not expecting.

**What you say:** "What do you have? I am happy to look at whatever it is."
**What you mean:** Some of my worst friends are my best enemies.
**Why this happens:** Manager has a piece of paper which will be read to you. Then you will have a chance to read it. You will not be given a copy. It will be put in your personal file. Any piece of paper given to you will not be put in an email, otherwise they would have emailed it to you in the first place.

Whatever Manager has decided to do about the situation has already been decided and approved by whomever approves whatever Manager does. You are being bought into this stew now just for the record, to say that they gave you a chance to comment and to stay out of legal trouble.

In this case, someone has targeted you with a memo or notice to Management about something you have done that has upset them or interfered with their next step.

Or, in all fairness to Manager, maybe you did do something.

In either case you have to listen and see what the notice is about.

**Is this a good sign you make the sale?** No. Everything is on hold until this situation is sorted out.
**What you do:** Nod. Say nothing you do not want repeated. Clam up.
**Boss?** No. Boss has already been made aware.

## The Situation – Explain

**Manager:** "Have you ever heard of this person/do you know this person?"
**Manager means:** No, you don't, and I know you don't.
**What you say:** "Can't say I have."
**What you mean:** I don't like a mystery.
**Why this happens:** Manager has decided that they are going to add someone to your crew. You will be working with someone on something at some point that you do not have affiliation with and whose agenda you have no idea about.

More importantly this person's loyalty is not with you. This is no secret to all involved.

You have been put in a transparent box for reasons that will not be revealed to you. It may or may not be performance related and if you ask you will be given a non-committal answer.

In contrast, this could be happening because Manager may have to put this person in a spot where they can watch them and form a next step around the results. And as a complement to you, they may trust you to work with this person.

The lesson is to look at both sides and do not make judgements until you see which way this new development plays out.

**Is this a good sign you will make the sale?** Yes, if this has nothing to do with you. No, if you are under review and they are watching you.

**What you do:** Nothing. Sell. Carry on. Take it in stride and let them see you taking it in stride.

**Boss?** No. Boss is in on it.


## The Situation – Explain

**Manager:** "Part of what we do around here is…"

**Manager means:** I have some policies/procedures/practices that are particular to me and my management style that are little off beat, so I have to wrap them in the larger Corporate culture to obscure the personal genesis of them.

**What you say:** "Always happy to learn!"

**What you mean:** I have enough to remember without having to memorize your unpublished Office Opus.

**Why this happens:** Some Managers are eccentric. Some Managers do not adhere, support, or abide by procedures, policies, and practices they do not agree with. Some Managers are trying new things to see how they go. Some Managers like to circumvent things to make their lives easier.

Either way, your Manager is your Manager and until you are the Manager you must go along with this. Incorporate the thing (and in this case it is usually a thing, not a series of things) as best you can unless it violates the law or Corporate policy.

Then again, it may not do any of these things and could be a different, more effective, or more efficient way of going about business.

**Is this a good sign you will make the sale?** Yes. This is not about your sale; it is about how you go about your day to day business at the Company.

**What you do:** Assess, review and tread softly.

**Boss?** Yes, only if it is illegal or out of line. Otherwise, no.

## The Situation – Explain

**Manager:** "I read your report."

**Manager means:** I read your report and I didn't like it.

**What you say:** "Great!"

**What you mean:** You, Manager, have tipped your hand.

**Why this happens:** When Manager likes your report, Manager delves right into what was liked about it. Manager will reference a specific section or thought or idea immediately. There is no need for a preamble to set up praise. The reason for that is there is no percentage in it for the Manager. Praise with preamble only sets up a conversation Manager does not want to have; the conversation where you ask for more money.

However, when Manager preambles by stating the obvious – the report was read – that is a set up line to make sure you understood that the firestorm of fault you are about to suffer is bracketed by the fact that the problem(s) surfaced when the whole thing was evaluated.

Choose to believe it or not. Could be that Manager only read up to the problematic part and considered that was enough, or the report was in fact read in its entirety. It does not make any difference. Your work is being flushed.

**Is this a good sign you will make the sale.** No.

**What you do:** Practice not saying anything by swallowing your tongue. This is useful lifelong skill for a career in Sales.

**Boss?** Yes. A good idea to see what you can do to avoid a repeat.

## The Situation – Explain

**Manager:** "This comes from the top."

**Manager means:** This is my decision, but I need cover to tell you.

**What you say:** "Alright then."

**What you mean:** I understand some things are beyond your control, and that is okay. But I don't believe it for a second, and we both know the truth, you stain on the carpet - what's it like living life always looking up through the crud?

**Why this happens:** The world is full of cowards. No Manager should hide behind another Manager for cover because the news about to be delivered is bad. Manager should own up to the news, discuss it transparently and outline Manager's role in the decision. Better for Manager to say Manager agreed or disagreed with the decision and how it will impact you rather than pretend the decision is out of Manager's control.

Afterall, if the decision is out of Manager's control, and that is admitted to, what good is Manager?

**Is this a good sign you will make the sale?** No.

**What you do:** Give it the silent treatment. Manager is already sweating telling you about the decision. Manager hates to sweat. Make it as hard as you can on Manager. Not only is Manager not your friend, Manager is useless. The sad thing is you both know it.

**Boss?** No. The Boss will find out about the silent treatment and be proud of you.

## The Situation – Explain

**Manager:** "We've reached a consensus."

**Manager means:** All of us agree you are not going to be given a choice, or be allowed to offer an opinion, on what I was told to tell you.

**What you say:** "Who is 'we?'"

**What you mean:** I am going to play dumb until you tell me who "we" is. I don't care about what you are going to tell me, I want to know who is doing the telling.

**Why this happens:** In some companies with many layers of redundant Management a herd mentality can develop and take over decision making. This may include decisions about you. Any herd likes to do things the easy way and this in turn includes making important decisions which can be bad or good for you.

**Is this a good sign you will make the sale:** Yes. If it took a committee to reach a decision it has nothing to do with sales. It has to do with something they want to tell you about something that will not impact the sale.

**What you do:** Don't get trampled.

**Boss?** No. It is all part of dealing with Managers.

## The Situation – Explain

**Manager:** "One of our Board members…"

**Manager means:** I got hung out to dry.

**What you say:** "Does the Board even knows who I am?"

**What you mean:** This is about shareholder value. And the Board does not value me as a Salesperson, even though I know the Board knows who I am by virtue of the fact you raised the Board as the source of whatever you are about to tell me.

**Why this happens:** Shareholder value has replaced profits as the main measure of Company success. A company, public or private, can fail miserably, fire everyone, close and evaporate – in effect show no profit and even lose tons of money – and the shareholder value will increase for some shareholders, most likely those shareholders on the Board of Directors.

"Shareholder value" as the main driver of corporate decision making is a cancer on free enterprise.

**Is this a good sign you will make the sale?** No. Something about you, or what you have been working on, caught a Board member's eye, and everything is on hold until it is sorted out to the Board member's satisfaction.

**What you do:** Look for work. If a Board member is reaching that far down into an organization to find you, something is very, very wrong.

**Boss?** No. Keep the Boss as your ally but look for work.

## The Situation – Explain

**Manager:** "I am of the opinion…"

**Manager means:** I am going to teach you something new now.

**What you say:** "It's always good to see things from another perspective."

**What you mean:** I'm going to learn something now.

**Why this happens:** Some people are born teachers or lecturers and they like to hold forth. This is not necessarily bad, it's just a fact. Some people use opinions to bend procedure and the longer Manager is in the same corporate strata, (Manager's place on the ladder,) the more opinions and procedure bending that person will do.

When Manager starts a conversation with an opinion the conversation is more about what Manager expects rather than what the Company needs. The "opinion" is a filter through which the larger corporate desire is processed through and what you are told is a distillation of Company goals and Manager requirements.

**Is this a good sign you will make the sale?** Yes. Manager has moved beyond your sale and does not care about revenue in this instance. Manager is desperate for an audience.

**What you do:** Clap.

**Boss?** No.

## The Situation – Explain

**Manager:** "Let me stop you there."

**Manager means:** Shut up.

**What you say:** "Okay."

**What you mean:** I know it when I hit a bridge abutment at one hundred miles per hour. How do I know? It hurts; like what you just said hurts. But you meant it to hurt, and I am not going to let on that it does. It is also uncalled for under any circumstances but especially at work.

**Why this happens:** Manager is a tyrant. No one should address a colleague in a business setting with that phrase. Manager is not your parent, or law enforcement or other authority figure outside of business.

**Is this a good sign you will make the sale:** No.

**What you do:** Listen to what comes next. You have been told to stop. You have stopped. Now there is silence. See what comes next. Most importantly, if you have your wits about you, write down exactly what Manager says. That act alone will make Manager crazy. Too bad. Didn't your mother teach you manners and not to talk to people that way?

**Boss?** Yes. Always report rudeness.

# 12

## Persuade

**Manager says:**

1) "Everyone has to be flexible."
2) "We are happy with your work"
3) "It's in our DNA."
4) "I could use your help."
5) "Well, what is your take on this?"
6) "The budget came up short. I need you to step up."
7) "It's your project if you want it."
8) "Let's figure this out together."
9) "What would you say if…".
10) "Think of this as a mission."

**Preparing for Persuade – Three things you need to have before you start:**

1) An open mind. Not everything someone is going to try to persuade you about may result in a negative outcome.

© Results Through Focus, LLC 2023
A. Berg, *Sales on the Go*, Business Guides on the Go,
https://doi.org/10.1007/978-1-0716-3211-6_12

2) Listen without prejudice. Hear what you do not want to hear and then form an opinion.
3) Be aware of what has been happening in and around the Company. Read the tea leaves if possible.

Persuasion, and the powers thereof, is a test of wills. There must be at least two people in any conversation and the person who is the best communicator usually gets what they want.

Not that all people who try to persuade you are out to get you. Quite the opposite can be true. Some people are working to point out to you what is in your best interest. Therefore enter so go a persuasion situation alert, calm, aware and confident in your ability to discern what is good for you, and what is bad for you.

Just know who you are dealing with as best you can and review your own personal position first before you come to judgement about what you hear.

## The Situation – Persuade

**Manager says:** "Everyone has to be flexible."
**Manager means:** You are about to get the short end of the stick.
**What you say:** "Absolutely! Everyone has to pitch in that way."
**What you mean:** I am going to hold you to "everyone," but I know a set up when I see one.
**Why this happens:** For some reason Manager believes you are the weak link in the chain, can be manipulated, bullied, coerced, hoodwinked, bamboozled, conned, or otherwise flimflammed into working twice as hard for half as much for twice as long in worse conditions as your associates.

This could be for the short term, or the long term. The point is you have been targeted. Rather than laying out your singular misfortune, Manager has to paint a broad mural of misery, suggesting that everyone is going to suffer, and the suffering is offered up as "flexibility."

You will never hear the word "flexibility" when good news is delivered. No one has to be "flexible" when they get a raise, or more responsibility, or a promotion. In a corporation, "flexibility" is always about getting less and doing more in half the time.

**Is this a good sign you will make the sale?** Yes, this time only. If you are not "flexible" you will never see another sale go forward if this Manager is involved.

**What you do:** In the short term – learn to Limbo. In the long term – look for work. The one thing about "flexibility" in a corporate setting is, most often, a permanent condition.

**Boss:** Yes. Inform Boss that you are working twice as hard for half as much for twice as long in a cesspool with bad lighting and no ventilation only if you find out that you are the only one being "flexible."

## The Situation – Persuade

**Manager says:** "We are happy with your work. What else can we do for you to get more out of you?"

**Manager means:** My baseline is your baseline, but I need to know what that is.

**What you say:** "Thanks for asking. Not to be greedy but I could really use XYZ."

**What you mean:** It is not often you ask what I would like beyond what I am getting now, and I am not going to take advantage of you, but there is something I could use.

**Why this happens:** Sometimes Manager and Management are in a true bind. This could be for reasons totally beyond their control. When you hear this question there is no agenda behind it. Manager needs your help to get more work done, needs it now, will give you more money or higher commission, and is not able to not to give you something to get out of whatever the bind is.

This is not bad, and Manager is not a bad person for asking this question. At least you are not being ordered to do something without any kind of acknowledgment or accommodation.

Keep in mind people who get greedy, or press their advantage in an organization, usually do not last too long. Never hold good fortune hostage.

**Is this a good sign you will make the sale:** Yes. Manager will move heaven and earth for you.
**What you do:** Whatever Manager needs. With a smile on your face and a song in your heart.
**Boss?** No. Manager knows you are magnanimous.

## The Situation – Persuade

**Manager says:** "It's in our DNA."
**Manager means:** I know science, and like science, DNA can't be changed.
**What you say:** "It's ingrained in everything we do."
**What you mean:** I know science too, but I also know that evolution is a science and things do change.
**Why this happens:** Manager is working to set you up for an explanation about something that is not quite right. This is neither a prelude to disaster nor good news. It is most likely something you can live with, but it will not sit well.

Manager is working hard to persuade you to accept whatever is happening with a minimum of fuss and bother.

The reference to DNA is the same as standing in front of a moving freight train. You cannot stop it and if you try you will be run over.

**Is this a good sign you will make the sale?** No. Something is up.
**What you do:** Make them come to you with whatever the endgame is. They hate that. Do not make it easy for them. Make them spit it out.
**Boss:** No. You are going to have to deal with it and seeing how it is not the end of the world, just listen, understand, and get on with it.

# The Situation – Persuade

**Manager:** "I could really use your help."
**Manager means:** I am going to inflate your ego before I ask you do something I should be doing but don't want to or can't.
**What you say:** "Of course, how can I help?"
**What you mean:** I am always helpful. I know that if someone asks for help and I decline, then I will not be asked to help again, and I do not want to miss out on what could be a great opportunity.
**Why this happens:** Manager may indeed need your help, so listen and help. Unless it is illegal or immoral or against Company policy, comply. You will make friends.

That said, catalog and then evaluate the type of help you have been asked to supply. Will you make new contacts, new friends, learn a new skill, engage with a department or executive you do not have a lot of exposure to, go to a new place, a new conference, tradeshow, or work with a new account?

Also, it's good to know people, such as yourself, have strengths and weaknesses. Asking for help takes courage.

It's not all bad.

**Is this a good sign you will make the sale?** Yes. And if you help Manager, many more if Manager has anything to say about it.
**What you do.** Comply. Help. Smile. Learn. Grow.
**Boss?** No. Boss will be told by Manager what a good person you are.

# The Situation – Persuade

**Manager:** "Well, what is your take on this?"
**Manager means:** I want your opinion for the record.
**What you say:** "I looked at this and my opinion is…"
**What you mean?** Was this omitted intentionally?

**Why this happens:** Manager wants input. Manager may be asking about something you have had time to ponder, or you may have been asked to respond to something that is a surprise. Either way, you are obligated to proffer an opinion.

Asking for an opinion can be a way for people to gather consensus or lay a trap. That is up to you to figure out, and probably easy to do if you have had history with Manager.

Know that people who are button pushers often ask for an opinion, see where you land on that subject, and then berate you in a passive aggressive manner to get a rise out of you.

Also know that Manager may value your insight and method of thought.

If you are unsure about the motive first offer a banal opinion, something general, that you would not mind being broadcast or printed, because it will be, seeing how your answer is on the record. If it is a trap, leave your opinion as general as you can. If it is a genuine consensus building exercise, give a detailed opinion that can optimize results for Manager.

Consider this as well; your opinion matters. You must have done something to earn Manager's respect enough to ask you.

**Is this a good sign you will make the sale?** Yes. An opinion solicited in this manner is not about the sale, it is about something else.

**What you do:** Give an opinion.

**Boss?** No. Not an issue. And if the opinion is a trap, you will have to deal with it.

## The Situation – Persuade

**Manager:** "The budget came up short. I need you to step up."

**Manager means:** I need help and I am putting you on the spot. Say "no;" I dare you.

**What you say:** "Of course. What's the situation?"

**What you mean:** (A) Why me? (B) Notice how I did not ask who fell short. (C) Notice I did not say "no." (D) What choice do I have? (E) You will owe me.

**Why this happens:** Manager may really need your help. Manager could be stress testing you. Manager could be signaling you that the person who came up short is on thin ice and Manager is looking for worthy candidates to assume more responsibility for more money. In any case you have no choice but to "step up."

**Is this a good sign you will make the sale?** Yes. Manager needs this sale. And the next. And the next. And the next.

**What you do:** Step up, gladly.

**Boss?** Yes. Stepping up may affect your day-to-day work and Boss will need to know that. But Boss will also understand you had no choice.


# The Situation – Persuade

**Manager:** "It's your project if you want it."
**Manager:** Take this off my hands, for better or worse.
**What you say:** "That's wonderful! I'll get started right away."
**What you mean:**

> If the project is toxic: I'll get my hazmat suit.
> If the project is a great opportunity: This could be my big break.
> If the project means I have to be smart: I got a 1600 combined score on my SATs.
> If the project is a career ender: I know all about the Titanic.

**Why this happens:**

> The project is toxic for Manager and will be toxic for you. Toxicity oozes downhill.
> The project is a prized plum. An audition for better things in the future.
> The project is a test. Let's see how you do.

**Is this a good sign you will make the sale?** Yes, provided you take on the project.

**What you do:** Get started and provide Manager with regular updates. Watch out for icebergs.

**Boss?** Yes. Boss needs to know how you stack up when confronted with different sorts of tests, both in terms of tolerance, talent, intelligence, and character.

## The Situation – Persuade

**Manager:** "Let's figure this out together."

**Manager means:** I know the outcome but let's see just how smart you really are.

**What you say:** "Alright, what's up?"

**What you mean:** No, thank you.

**Why this happens:** You are about to get sucked into a corporate vortex on some issue that is causing consternation somewhere. You are not involved but Manager has decreed your intellect and career will be cannon fodder for whatever happens going forward.

However, Manager wants to memorialize your input as fingerprint proof Manager engaged with someone who is not a stakeholder in the matter and who can be sacrificed if the thing goes sideways. Manager was never going to be "together" with you on this situation. You are for all intents and purposes, alone.

**Is this a good sign you will make the sale?** No. Your deal will be held hostage unless and until you do the "figure out" part for Manager.

**What you do:** Provide as little meaningful input as possible and run as far and as fast as you can away from the situation. Practice "double talk" and "gibberish" in the mirror. There is no upside when Manager asks for input in this manner. It's code for Armageddon – your Armageddon.

**Boss?** No. Deal with it as best you can.

## The Situation – Persuade

**Manager:** "What would you say if…"
**Manager means:** I know something you don't.
**What you say:** "I'll listen to anything."
**What you mean:** Nothing is hypothetical if I must answer for something.
**Why this happens:** Manager is using the hypothetical to mask reality. The actual situation in question is real, it is not a theory or a role-play. It has happened, is happening, or will happen.

You are being asked to react to a real thing couched as a hypothetical because the actual thing is sensitive, and to ask you to comment on something real, and sensitive, would upset a lot of people, most likely you. Hence, the false feeling of protection and comfort provided by declaring whatever it is as "hypothetical."
Do not be fooled.

**Is this a good sign you will make the sale.** Yes, but only if you know your quantum physics and play the game.
**What you do:** After you comment on the situation by declaring your answer "hypothetical" (you might as well play the game), ask if the hypothetical is a real thing. Gauge the reaction – the truth will be in Manager's eyes.
**Boss?** No. Learn how to conjugate theory, antithesis, and synthesis and you can fathom any hypothesis.

## The Situation – Persuade

**Manager:** "Think of it as a mission."
**Manager means:** I am volunteering you for a dangerous mission.
**What you say:** "Saddle up!"
**What you mean:** You've got to be kidding.
**Why this happens:** This is not just any mission. It is a suicide mission. Most times you get to volunteer to go on a suicide mission. Not in Manager's mindset. You are expendable, hence the military analogy. You have been ordered to volunteer.

**Is this a good sign you will make the sale?** Yes, seeing how Manager is sacrificing you for something. Think of this deal as your last meal.

**What you do:** Ask for special compensation in regard to this mission. Or order a steak.

**Boss?** No. It is all part of playing the Corporate game.

# 13

## Direct

**Manager says:**

1) "Okay, let's get started."
2) "We are going to have a kick-off meeting."
3) "Put on your thinking caps."
4) "I want you onboard with this."
5) "When you drill down…."
6) "Take a step back for a moment."
7) "Paint a bigger picture."
8) "Look at the optics."
9) "Think it through logically."
10) "Apply a process to the effort."

**Preparing for Direct – Three things you need to have before you start:**

1) Previous marketing plans for any project, if available.
2) Any company promotional materials or advertisements.
3) Company handbook.

© Results Through Focus, LLC 2023
A. Berg, *Sales on the Go*, Business Guides on the Go,
https://doi.org/10.1007/978-1-0716-3211-6_13

This section focuses on how the company sets expectations, begins the sales process, and orders assets to be effective going forward.

Therefore, the best way to be ready for this interlude is to be aware of previous plans, the results of those plans so you can see the public facing results, and the policies the company may have in terms of working the mission statement into the company's products.

Always remember; You cannot escape the past so you might as well learn from it. Past is prelude.

## The Situation – Direct

**Manager:** "Okay, let's get started."

**Manager means:** Listen to my orders. Here they come.

**What you say:** "Got my coffee!"

**What you mean:** I am always ready to start and always on my way. I don't need to be reminded.

**Why this happens:** Manager is organized at the least and may be a control freak at the most. But there is nothing wrong with being a control freak about time at work. After all, time is money.

Manager understands simple process – there is a beginning, middle and end, and you must start someplace. This is Manager's style, and it is not going to change.

This is a good Manager. Manager may be a little rough when it comes to direction but any Manager that gets things done and makes you money is a good person to be around.

**What you do:** Set your watch. Finish your coffee. Watch and learn from the process.

**Is this a good sign you will make the sale?** Yes. You already are organized and disciplined. Manager will enjoy working with you.

**Boss?** No. Let Boss enjoy the day.

## The Situation – Direct

**Manager:** "We are going to have a kick-off meeting."
**Manager:** I like to waste time.
**What you say:** "Great!"
**What you mean:** I will show up with two ideas if you call on me to speak.
**Why this happens:** Kick-off meetings are a ritual. Like brain-storming sessions, they are designed to fill a block of time on the corporate calendar, show upper management that something is happening even if nothing is getting done and forces people with better more productive things to do to gather in a room and stare at the clock on the wall.
Kick-off meetings are a corporate requisite when involving more than one department is involved. Marching orders are disseminated in the planning stages and the kick-off meeting is a gathering of the tribe – a new tribe for sure – but still a tribe.
**Is this a good sign you will make the sale:** Yes. Only if you show up for the kick-off meeting.
**What you do:** Do not kick up your feet up on the table at the kick-off meeting.
**Boss?** No. Kick-off meetings are a fact of corporate life. Learn to enjoy bagels and muffins.

## The Situation – Direct

**Manager:** "Put on your thinking caps."
**Manager means:** I have no idea what I am doing and have to revert to language teachers use in the third grade.
**What you say:** "Right."
**What you mean:** Stop treating me like a child you incompetent buffoon.
**Why this happens:** When this phrase is used it means Manager must resort to grade school language because Manager never learned Management skills. This is the best Manager can muster and it is indicative of the level Manager works at.

**Is this a good sign you will make the sale?** Yes. If only because Manager has no idea what a "sale" is.

**What you do:** Participate so that people see you are part of this group. Impart nothing of import or consequence. Offer no wisdom. Do not be an impediment, however. Senior Management will weed this goof ball out soon enough.

**Boss.** No. Boss knows a moron when Boss sees one.

## The Situation – Direct

**Manager:** "I want you onboard with this."

**Manager means:** This is an order.

**What you say:** "I am on board for sure!"

**What you mean:** I know an order when I hear one and will comply even if I do not know what I am being ordered to do.

**Why this happens:** Manager runs a tight ship. Nothing wrong with that. Manager deploys assets as Manager sees fit. Nothing wrong with that. This could be good as Manager is results focused and sees you as part of the plan.

The style might be a little harsh, but Managers are entitled to their styles, and you can learn a lot about the world from being exposed to different styles.

Furthermore, you can follow these orders because they are not about doing something illegal, immoral or against Company policy. If that were the case you would not be ordered, you would be cajoled, bamboozled, or gently prodded.

**What you do:** Do as you are told. Keep an open mind. Let any harsh style wash over you.

**Boss?** No.

## The Situation – Direct

**Manager:** "When you drill down..."

**Manager means:** I have to find fault with what you did. However, you posted excellent results on this project and therefore any faults are not readily apparent. Therefore, I have to look microscopically at the data to find something I can pin on you and knock your commission down to within my budget for additional compensation.

**What you say:** "The data is the data no matter how you look at it."

**What you mean:** You cheap coward.

**Why this happens:** "Drilling down" only happens when there is an unexpected result that is going to cost Manager money.

Nobody "drills down" to find good news or more money for you.

The phrase "drilling down" is meant to examine each piece of data on its own, not as part of an aggregate whole. In this exercise Manager will find something in your deal that is not in compliance. Then Manager can reduce your commission.

Of course, the Company will keep the revenue, but pay you as little as possible. Your sin is you were too successful, and the commission Manager has to pay you exceeds what was budgeted. In turn, because your commission exceeds the commission budget, Manager's forecasting skills will be suspect.

**What you do:** Fight every step of the way. Challenge every assertion associated with reducing your commission. Make this as uncomfortable for Manager as possible. Manager is a coward. By fighting every assertion during the "drill drown" you will help ensure Manager does not "drill down" into your stuff again.

**Boss?** Yes. Let Boss know you made the Company money fair and square, and Manager is trying to reduce your commission to save Manager's neck.

## The Situation – Direct

**Manager:** "Take a step back for a moment."

**Manager means:** I am wrong, and you are right, but I need to convince you that I am right, and you are wrong.

**What you say:** "Go ahead."

**What you mean:** I will give you the courtesy of being heard because I have to work with you, but I am not going to cede ground.

**Why this happens:** When Manager asks you to "take a step back for a moment," Manager is trying to get you to see Manager's point of view which supports Manager's position as opposed to yours.

Manager must correct the record in Manager's favor. Whatever you have done has gone against something Manager was doing, or tasked to do, or interfered with a pre-determined outcome. The only way to make an adjustment in Manager's favor is to have you reconsider your position.

Thus, the phasing of "stepping back." "Stepping back" provides a new and different perspective Manager is going to ask you to accept and thus the results will be more in line with Manager's expectations.

**Is this a good sign you will make the sale?** No. It is in jeopardy in this instance.

**What you do:** Consider if this is a sword you want to fall on. It's up to you.

**Boss?** Yes. Re-affirm your work, your position on the subject and your course of action.


## The Situation – Direct

**Manager:** "Let me paint a bigger picture for you."
**Manager means:** You are not seeing the whole picture.
**What you say:** "Tell me more."
**What you mean:** Thank you.
**Why this happens.** This is really good, and it is as rare as it is really good. Manager will impart hard-won wisdom and insight to you because while you have done a good job, by listening to Manager, you can do a better job and earn more money.
**Is this a good sign you will make the sale?** Yes. If this is not obvious in this case, nothing is obvious.
**What you do:** Follow Manager's instructions and hang on this person.
**Boss?** No. This is good news. Boss may have had a hand in it, too.


## The Situation – Direct

**Manager:** "Look at the optics."

**Manager means:** Don't focus on the results, focus on the process.

**What you say:** "I see what you mean."

**What you mean:** Explain it to me.

**Why this happens:** When Manager can't get things done, Manager concentrates on process. Working a process creates a lot of energy, vibration, smoke, and noise, but no results. "Optics" is what something looks like through a different lens. In this case "Optics" is the lens of process.

Manager is asking you to reassess what you have done from a process point of view rather than a results point of view. The advantage to Manager is if you can reframe your results in terms of how something looks rather than what was accomplished. In so doing you can either make Manager look better or cover up some failing of Manager.

"Optics" is code for "make me look good and I will leave you alone."

**Is this a good sign you will make the sale.** Yes. This time.

**What you do:** Memorialize the results and then dress it up any way the Manager wants provided you look good, too.

**Boss?** No. Don't bore Boss with Manager's insecurities.

## The Situation – Direct

**Manager:** "Think it through logically."

**Manager means:** You are missing a few steps in the process, and you can do better.

**What you say:** "Walk me through it."

**What you mean:** If I missed something I want to learn what that was for now, and the future.

**Why this happens:** It is all good. Manager sees you can do the job and wants to extract more upside in your deal if you can think things through a little differently.

Thinking differently could be taking more care to observe your deal making environment, absorbing other points of view, listening more carefully to others, and otherwise keeping your head on a swivel.

Manager wants to take time to walk you through your process through Manager's eyes and ears. Take advantage of this lesson.

**Is this a good sign you will make the sale?** Yes. And you will learn in the process.

**What you do:** Take careful notes and apply the advice to the situation.

**Boss?** No. No need.

## The Situation – Direct

**Manager:** "Apply a process to the effort."

**Manager means:** Good job, but bad style.

**What you say:** "What other steps are needed?"

**What you mean:** How can I dress this up better to satisfy the corporate culture even though the results are great?

**Why this happens:** Some organizations reward Managers for style over substance. This is especially true where an organization acquires business and derives revenue from the way it presents itself, how it handles customers and clients and otherwise provides a "look" that people will pay for.

Therefore, if you show up with great revenue, but the deal is rough around the edges somehow, you will be asked to adhere to the organization's "process" next time you put together a deal.

This "process" could be the way you dress, where you take a customer to lunch, what time of day you follow-up, and other subtle nuances that make up style. Rather than ask you to adjust your style, which may run afoul of HR rules, by cloaking "style" in "process," Manager can achieve the desired result, and everyone is happy.

Except you, if you do not buy into, or comport with, the corporate style.

**Is this a good sign you will make the sale?** Yes.

**What you do:** Take the time and make the effort to learn what the "process" is and incorporate it into your "style." Afterall, it is go along to get along world sometimes.

**Boss?** No. Your adjustment to the "process" will be evolutionary and under your control.

# 14

## Review

**Manager says:**

1) "I'll get right to the point."
2) "You've got great potential."
3) "How do you feel the project went?"
4) "The facts are conclusive."
5) "Sit down."
6) "This is a good review."
7) (Clearing throat) – Bad sign.
8) "I've spoken with the Board/Partners/Executive Committee."
9) "The Company has hired a Management Consultant."
10) "We've invited some investors to come in."

**Preparing for Review – Three things you need to have before you start:**

1) Your sales result to date.
2) Correspondence that puts you in a good light.
3) Evidence of results; advertisements, samples, media coverage.

© Results Through Focus, LLC 2023
A. Berg, *Sales on the Go*, Business Guides on the Go,
https://doi.org/10.1007/978-1-0716-3211-6_14

Manager will have your sales results from Accounting. So will you. Make sure the data matches. Never rely on data supplied by Manager to you, only rely on data from Accounting. If you can't get your data from Accounting (some companies don't allow you direct asses to your own data), go with your own, and challenge any data from any other source not in your favor. Make them do a side-by-side compare of your data and Accounting's data, that way you will see their data.

Collect and catalog complimentary correspondence from accounts, customers, supplies and colleagues no matter how trivial. In this case volume means more than content.

Your product only produces revenue when it sells. Have evidence of your sales at hand.

## The Situation – Review

**Manager:** "I'll get right to the point."
**Manager means:** Bad news.
**What you say:** "Okay."
**What you mean:** I'll react when I'm ready.
**Why this happens:** Manager does not waste time, pulls punches, or sugar coats anything. Maybe Manager would not have had a good career as a diplomat; business is not about diplomacy – it is about getting things done.
There is nothing wrong with this approach. Remember that if you perform and keep your nose clean, you will not hear this unless whatever the bad news is has nothing to do with you. This is a good Manager. Manager values time and honesty. Not a bad combination even if this particular circumstance is not good for you.
In that case, the bad news is more corporate than individual; a downsizing, purchase, re-organization, etc.
Don't take it personally, unless it is.
**Is this a good sign you will make the sale?** No.
**What you do:** Absorb it and move on.
**Boss?** No. Boss is already aware.

## The Situation – Review

**Manager:** "You've got great potential."
**Manager means:** But you are not living up to it.
**What you say:** "I am glad you see potential in me."
**What you mean:** But, but, but.
**Why this happens:** Mangers who use this phrase generally fall into two groups:

> 1) The Mentor Type – Manager has you on the team because Manager finds your skill set useful. You have performed well, but could perform better, and Manager feels it incumbent upon Manager to point out what you did well and what you could do better. Manager wants the team to succeed. This is a good Manager.
> 2) The Goal Post Mover – Manager keeps people on edge and off balance by moving the metrics of success. This is a classic way to keep people in line by making them guess about what needs to be done, a way to always deliver unwarranted criticism, and reduce commissions and other upsides. Manger uses work to play internal mental games. This is a bad Manager.

**Is this a good sign you will make the sale?** 1) Yes. 2) No.
**What you do:** 1) Listen, take notes, adjust for next time. 2) Zone out because you will never win.
**Boss?** 1) No. 2) Yes. Boss needs to know you are being set up to fail because the goal posts keep moving.

## The Situation – Review

**Manager:** "How do you feel the project went?"
**Manager means:** I know the answer. I want to see if we are on the same page.
**What you say:** "It went great!"

**What you mean:** You are never going to get me to admit to anything less than "Great!" when you ask me this open-ended question that I know, you know, the answer to.

**Why this happens:** Lawyers who do not work for you never ever ask a question they do not already know the answer to. In the same vein, Manager never asks a team member "how a project went" unless they know the answer.

Be guided by that fact. Manager knows the answer. Manager does not care how you feel about the project. Manager wants to know if the project met your expectations or not and then determine if you can be trusted on Manager's next project.

**Is this a good sign you will make the sale?** No. Something is up.

**What you do:** Be precise in your answer.

**Boss?** No. Handle this yourself.

## The Situation – Review

**Manager:** "The facts are conclusive."

**Manager means:** My facts are the true facts regardless of the facts.

**What you say:** "let's look at the facts, then."

**What you mean:** Your facts may not be my facts, but the facts are the facts.

**Why this happens:** Manager may want to present skewed and/or biased conclusions based on raw, unfiltered, and irrefutable facts. The reason is Manager' skewed/bias interpretations of the facts will contaminate whatever the next steps may be in someone else's best interest(s) but certainly not yours.

By itself, relying on the facts is good – you rely on the facts to present your sales results for example.

**Is this a good sign you will make the sale?** Yes. Presentation of facts – pure or not – is offered post-sale. What is at stake is what happens next.

**What you do:** Know your facts as true facts. Keep everything simple. Facts are rarely if ever, complicated.

**Boss?** No. You do not need Boss to interpret the facts.

## The Situation – Review

**Manager:** "Sit down."
**Manager means:** This is really, really, bad.
**What you say:** "Sure."
**What you mean:** This is going to be horrible for me.
**Why this happens:** Whatever the news is, it is catastrophic for you. Manager has been through this before and has been advised by Legal and HR that before delivering any world-ending news to an associate to have them sit down before proceeding and do not proceed unless and until they do.

The reason for this is simple. When horrendous news is delivered to people, it is common for people to faint. Legal and HR cannot have a situation at work where bad news is delivered, the associate faints, and hurts themselves in the fall. This fall will result in a lawsuit and workman compensation claims. Legal and HR do not care about how you feel. They just want you to walk out the door in one piece. Manager may care about how you feel, but the command to "sit down" has nothing to do with Manager.

Asking you to sit down is not a humanitarian gesture. It simply protects the bottom line. And if you were in the same position, you would do the same thing. It's not personal, it's business.

**Is this a good sign you will make the sale?** Yes. Surprisingly yes. Manager will let the sale go through and pay you your commission so there is no trouble going forward. But you are finished and done at this Company.
**What you do.** Sit down and try not to sweat through your clothes.
**Boss?** No. Boss will provide good references.

## The Situation – Review

**Manager:** "This is a good review."
**Manager means:** I have good news.
**What you say:** "That's wonderful to hear!"
**What you mean:** That's a relief.

**Why this happens:** Sometimes good news is just that – good news. There is no hidden agenda. Furthermore, the phrase "good news" means there is consensus about the good news at every level above Manager and whatever the fallout is for you it has been sanctioned and signed off on at the highest levels.

**Is this a good sign you will make the sale:** Yes.

**What you do:** Sit back and enjoy it.

**Boss?** Yes. Thank Boss for the support and encouragement.


## The Situation – Review

**Manager:** (Clearing throat) – Bad sign.

**Manager means:** I need a momentary pause before I speak to you.

**What you say:** "Are you alright?"

**What you mean:** You are such a bad actor.

**Why this happens:** Manager signals unwelcome news or developments with body language. Because Manager is delivering non-optimal news to you verbally and has probably used up all the stock phrases that presage bad news with you at some time in the past, the throat clearing sound signals something important is about to be communicated.

Clearing the throat preps the vocal cords to produce the purest sound possible. It also gives the brain a chance to review the next steps and how the next steps will be presented.

Whatever it is, it is not good. People in general will clear their throats when addressing a group, but this is for purposes of projecting their voice as far and as clearly as possible. When done in a close setting, such as an office, throat clearing is acting.

**Is this a good sign you will make the sale?** No. The sale is dead.

**What you do:** Hear Manager out without reacting.

**Boss?** No. Bad news is normal in life and business.

## The Situation – Review

**Manager:** "I've spoken with the Executive Committee."

**Manager means:** I do not have the authority on my own to tell you about what is going to happen next, and so glad I do not.

**What you say:** "Who are they? I've never met them."

**What you mean:** If you are going to run under their skirts as cover, I am calling you out for the weakling that you are and make this as hard as possible.

**Why this happens:** Weaklings will do as weaklings will. Either Manager went to the Executive Committee with a difficult thing to tell you about and wanted the Committee to act as cover, or the Executive Committee came to the Manager with the difficult thing and wanted the Manager to act as cover for them.

Either way you are working with weaklings and cowards. If there is bad news, you want to work with people who can deliver the bad news professionally, upfront, look you in the eye, offer to shake your hand, just as they would deliver good news.

Furthermore, Executive Committees do not deal in good news. Executive Committees were formed ages ago to spread the liability for bad news across as many people as possible to provide deniability on an individual basis. An Executive Committee is a firing squad without guns.

**Is this a good sign you will make the sale?** No. Maybe you will get some form of payout, but the deal is dead or reassigned.

**What you do:** Demand a written explanation. You won't get it, but demand it verbally and then follow-up in writing.

**Boss?** No. Even the Boss has a Boss.

## The Situation – Review

**Manager:** "The Company has hired a Management Consultant."

**Manager means:** No one is safe. Heads up.

**What you say:** "That's never good."

**What you mean:** You can't fool me.

**Why this happens:** Any top to bottom review of a Company from an outside consultant is driven by the Board of Directors, the Executive Committee, investors, or Legal. There is no reason to hire a Management Consultant if everything is going well.

There is no negotiating with a Management Consultant. The Consultant has been told to find for a pre-determined result. The report will act as cover. It does not matter what anyone at the Company does or says. Just about everyone or anyone can or will be fired.

**Is this a good sign you will make the sale?** Yes. Every deal you make will be approved to glean every cent out of you before you are canned.

**What you do.** Close as many deals as possible before the balloon goes up, or the axe comes down. Make them come to you with the Exit Package in writing and don't quit unless you have another job.

**Boss?** No. It's endgame.


## The Situation – Review

**Manager:** "We've invited some investors to come in."
**Manager means:** We have traded control for money.
**What you say:** "Are they going to invest in me?"
**What you mean:** How much are they investing and how much control is Management giving up?
**Why this happens:**

1) The Company needs the money due to bad Management, is in trouble and only an infusion of capital can correct the problem.

2) The Company sees growth opportunities and does not have the capital to take advantage of market conditions to expand, open new accounts and stay ahead of the competition.

3) The Company was about to be purchased by bad people and the Company invited investors in to prevent that.

Either way, the investors are now running the show. Even if they do not have a majority stake, they know how to make a lot of noise, make people nervous, and otherwise throw their weight around.

What you can count on is they know nothing about what you or the Company does but will tell you how to do things anyway because they are rich and think they know more than you do by virtue of their wealth.

**Is this a good sign you will make the sale?** Yes. Investors do not care about sales; they care about control.

**What you do:** Just go about your business.

**Boss?** No. This is not news to Boss.

# 15

## Reward (or Not)

**Manager says:**

1. "I wish it was more."
2. "Here is your raise and bonus."
3. "The Company did not perform to budget/plan/expectation."
4. "This is not what you were expecting."
5. "We pay for results, and you delivered."
6. "Remember, compensation matters are confidential."
7. "HR is joining us."
8. "Sorry for the delay setting this up."
9. "What do you feel you should get."
10. "We want you to be happy."

**Preparing for Reward – Three things you need to have before you start:**

1. Your Employment Contract if you have one.
2. Reviews of the Company's compensation information from outside sources.

© Results Through Focus, LLC 2023
A. Berg, *Sales on the Go*, Business Guides on the Go,
https://doi.org/10.1007/978-1-0716-3211-6_15

3.  A short list of new resources you want to include going forward. These would include new territories, new categories to work in, or whatever else you need which will give you access to more and better deals.

Having your contract at hand, in a folder, on your lap, tells Manager you are ready to engage. Manager has your contract on Manager's desk. You having your contract makes it an even playing field.

Outside reviews of compensation are considered leaked information. This makes Manager and Management nuts. Too bad.

Your Wish List is not about creature comforts. It is about how you can leverage your worth to find more and bigger deals, make more money and make yourself invaluable to the Company.

## The Situation – Reward (or Not)

**Manager:** "I wish it was more."
**Manager means:** I did the best I could for you.
**What you say:** "Thank you. This is very much appreciated, and I know you did everything you could for me."
**What you mean:** I know you did the best you could, thank you.
**Why this happens:** Manager did indeed do all the Manager could to get you the best raise or upside available. Manager uses this phrase to emphasize that your work is highly valued by the Manager, but Manager was constrained by forces beyond Manager's control to get you the true amount you deserved.
This is from the heart. The Manager will get you more as soon as possible.
**Is this a good sign you will make the sale?** Yes.
**What you do:** Accept whatever is offered with grace and gratitude. Stay close to Manager. This is a good Manager not so much because Manager got you more money, but because Manager saw the good in you. That is way more valuable in the long run than any raise or bonus.
**Boss?** No. You got all that you could get this go-round.

## The Situation – Reward (or Not)

**Manager:** "Here is your raise and bonus."

**Manager means:** You got what you deserved, and I want you to know I am the sole reason you got it; not because you worked hard for it, but because I control you.

**What you say:** "This is wonderful. Thank you."

**What mean:** I got what I deserved because I earned it. You did not give it to me.

**Why this happens:** Some people do not give with an open hand. Some people can only give when they hold something back. Some people cannot give because they have nothing to give as a personality, and when they are charged with giving our raises and bonuses in a corporate setting, they have to perform this act as a "pass through" – that is – they have to give you something even as the act of giving makes them uncomfortable or anxious.

Manager is not the sole reason you got your deserved increase; you are. If you had underperformed the conversation would be quite different.

**Is this a good sign you will make the sale?** Yes. This has nothing to do with you.

**What you do:** Accept the good news with a smile and handshake. Make a note about the personality you are dealing with.

**Boss?** No. Boss knows there is a pot of gold at the end of the rainbow.

## The Situation – Reward (or Not)

**Manager:** "The Company did not perform to budget/plan/expectation."

**Manager means:** We are going to bleed you dry.

**What you say:** "That's disturbing. What can I do to help?"

**What you mean:** You and I know I performed but others did not, and I know you are setting me up for no raise or upside, or even a pay cut. By offering to help I signal that I am a team player as I even look for work.

**Why this happens:** When you work for anyone other than yourself you are at the mercy as to how the organization performs and in turn how you are compensated. On the other hand, if the Company does well, and you are not doing as well as you would like, you may benefit from corporate largess and keep your job.

Assess why the Company is not doing as well, this will determine if you can ride it out and wait for better conditions, or the problems may be systemic to the Company in which case you may need to get out of there.

**Is this a good sign you will make the sale?** Yes. The Company needs every deal it can get.

**What you do.** See what the next sentence is. Ask for details around the poor performance and ferret out if it is market conditions or corporate incompetence.

**Boss?** No. There is nothing Boss can do.


# The Situation – Reward (or Not)

**Manager:** "This is not what you were expecting."

**Manager means:** We are going to give you less than what was promised by plan and take the risk you will not leave over this issue.

**What you say:** "I'm listening."

**What you mean:** I am not going to tip my hand just yet by giving you any sort of reaction you can judge my next steps by.

**Why this happens:** In the cruel calculus of corporate compensation, Manager will come up with a formula to give you less than you deserve, but just enough to keep you from leaving. If you can examine this gap between what is deserved and what you will tolerate you will see just how complex a formula this is.

Manager has considered your past record; are you a top earner, on the bubble, up and coming, over the hill, coasting, hustling, a lone wolf, a collaborator, a saboteur, a team player, a firebrand, or push over. All these observations go into an algorithm uniquely yours.

The amount of money Manager is short on will be enough to help Manager make Manager's budget and at the same time enough to keep you in line and show up for work tomorrow.

Unless you act otherwise.

**Is this a good sign you will make the sale?** Yes. No use in rubbing salt into the wound.

**What you do.** Take the money. Go home, think about it. Ball is in your court.

**Boss?** Yes. Discuss the gap and see what Boss thinks.

## The Situation – Reward (or Not)

**Manager:** "We pay for results, and you delivered."

**Manager means:** Thank you, thank you, thank you.

**What you say:** "This is a great place to work and thank you for the opportunity."

**What you mean:** Thank you, thank you, thank you.

**Why this happens:** Sometimes good news is simply that; good news.

**Is this a good sign you will make the sale?** Yes.

**What you do:** Say thank you, accept whatever is given to you in the form that it is given, talk about a bright future and mean every word of it. This is a good Manager.

**Boss?** Yes. Thank Boss.

## The Situation – Reward (or Not)

**Manager:** "Remember, compensation matters are confidential."

**Manager means:** You are about to get way more than you expected.

**What you say:** "Of course, that is way it should be."

**What you mean:** I play be the rules. Now, lay it on me.

**Why this happens:** Manager recognizes your above-and-beyond contribution and has arranged a wonderful new compensation package for you. However, it is extraordinary in some regards and will make your associates upset if they find out about it.

Therefore, Manager is enlisting your cooperation to keep this matter confidential even though the Company manual tells you that. It is just a reminder, but it also something else.

When you are reminded of a Company policy you know very well, the emphasis is meant to communicate you are being singled out for some reason. In this case the reminder of confidentiality is based on something good. But, next time maybe not. Be on the lookout for Company policy callouts as preambles to conversation specific to you.

**What you do:** Accept this gift. Spend it in another city. Keep your mouth shut.

**Boss?** No. Technically you cannot say anything. Boss will respect you play by this rule because Boss knows anyway.

## The Situation – Reward (or Not)

**Manager:** "HR is joining us."
**Manager means:** I called for reinforcements.
**What you say:** "Alright with me."
**What you mean:** Bring it.
**Why this happens:** Never, ever think HR is there for you. HR is there to protect the Company, not you. They may administer benefits, but they do not do so because they care about you.

When HR joins Manager, HR is there to quote policy, line by line. Manager will outline the picture, and HR will fill in the details. Also, HR functions as a witness. Nothing ever good comes of HR joining a meeting. The only good thing is you have gotten the warning.

In some cases, when you show up to a meeting and HR already there, and you weren't expecting them, it's bad, really bad. When HR and Legal surprise you in a meeting with Manager you are not only fired, but you are also being shown the door immediately.

**Is this a good sign you will make the sale?** Yes. Whatever you have done in sales will be commissioned as per plan. You have been frozen out of anything new until whatever HR is concerned about is resolved to HR's satisfaction.

**What you do:** Say as little as possible. Admit to nothing. If they show you evidence, do not comment. If the decision is to fire you, then the decision was made previously, and HR wants to gauge reaction. If you comment or react at all it will be used against you. No comment and no reaction means you were tipped off, or you are beyond their control, which you are because you are a Salesperson and always in control. Either way this will make them crazy with anxiety. If you have been fired and shown the door, go home and call your attorney.

**Boss?** No. Boss is aware, unfortunately.

## The Situation – Reward (or Not)

**Manager:** "Sorry for the delay in setting this up."

**Manager means:** I had to fight for what I am about to give you but don't want to tell you that.

**What you say:** "No need to apologize; we all have a lot to do."

**What you mean:** I am chill.

**Why this happens:** Manager had to navigate difficult and complicated waters to get you this new compensation package. Along the way Manager encountered resistance from people you probably work with every day and have some say in what you should get. Hence the delay.

The upside here is Manager fought for you in a steady and quiet fashion. At every step of the way Manager was able to convince the other parties or overcome the objections.

**Is this a good sign you will make the sale?** Yes.

**What you do:** Thank Manager, take what is given, and reiterate you understand the delay and it was no problem. By saying this you will acknowledge to Manager that you knew Manager went out on limb for you without saying it.

**Boss?** Yes. Just tell Boss that Manager came through and the delay was not Manager's fault.

## The Situation – Reward (or Not)

**Manager:** "What do you feel you should get?."

**Manager means:** I like to play children's games.

**What you say:** "Whatever works for you."

**What you mean:** You tell me first.

**Why this happens:** This is the classic no-win scenario. The Manager is like the dealer in Blackjack. Only the Manager knows what cards Manager is holding. Manager knows your compensation package and wants to know where you think you should be in terms of income based on your work.

If you quote a number higher than that which Manager has for you, you will not get it and Manager knows you value your work higher than Manager does.

If you quote a number lower than Manager has for you – presto – you have that lower number and Manager returns the difference to Manager's budget.

Manager cannot lose. Only you can lose. Like in Blackjack over the long term.

**Is this a good sign you will make the sale?** Yes. Manager gets the money either way.

**What you do:** Do not give Manager a number. Sit there and let Manager waste Manager's time. You have no place to go until you get Manager's number.

**Boss?** No. This is typical juvenile behavior on the part of Manager.


## The Situation – Reward (or Not)

**Manager:** "We want you to be happy."

**Manager means:** What can we do for you that does not involve money.

**What you say:** "That is kind of you. There is one thing I could use…."

**What you mean:** I get it, you want to make my life easier without it costing you more in salary or commission. It cannot be a leased car or a bigger office or bigger, better accounts. Here is my one thing….

**Why this happens:** This is very benign and is meant as a small stakes gesture. Manager cannot get you a life changing new compensation package but wants you to know you are valued, and can be granted a small token of appreciation.

There is no big raise and special bonus in the offing when you hear this phrase. Such a development would be presented differently. If you reach for the Moon, you will be denied, and Manager will think you are greedy.

**Is this a good sign you will make the sale?** Yes. This has nothing to do with sales.

**What you do:** Ask for a new office chair. Manager loves that. You are more comfortable; it is in Manager's budget and a symbol to others you got something shiny and new.

**Boss?** No. Small stakes; don't bother.

# Sales on The Go – Flowchart

Now that you have gone through the three sections of the book; Sales, Marketing and Management, the process, and thinking guiding the process, is basically the same for each section.

After all, Sales is just Sales. There is no magic.

The following flowchart shows the process in two dimensions. The "Them" is a catch-all for Buyer, Marketer and Manager. The long vertical lines separate the External and Internal thinking of Them and You. Everything You hear and think and everything They hear and think happens in the Internal section. All spoken words and actions take place in the External section.

As you will see, most of the External and Internal action happens on the "You" side of the page. This is because you are initiating action, listening for replies and cues, spooling up your next set of assessments and actions, and then moving them forward. Most of the heavy lifting for getting the sale is your responsibility and therefore confers a bias on you to succeed.

© Results Through Focus, LLC 2023
A. Berg, *Sales on the Go*, Business Guides on the Go,
https://doi.org/10.1007/978-1-0716-3211-6

Sales on the Go

Sales Process Flowchart

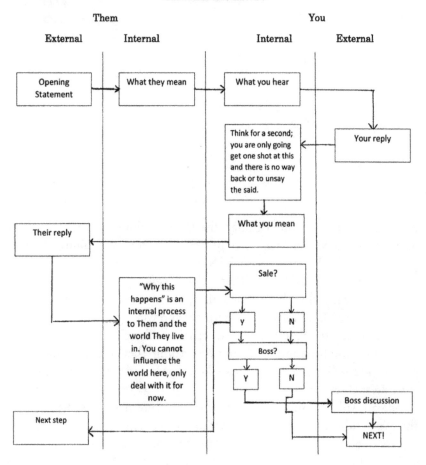

# The Final Close

Well, what did you think?

Contact me here: resultstf@gmail.com

If you got this far then you know what I know: sales and selling is the most fun you will ever have in business, and possibly in life.

I feel this way because in my sales life I have met the most wonderful people, done the most exciting things, learned about subjects I had no idea even existed, gained insights into what were once mysteries, traveled all over and learned everywhere is great no matter how far away or how close, told my stories, listened to other's stories and gained a specific and special confidence to move throughout the world that I do not believe can be available to anyone who does not sell.

This just my opinion. A life in sales can also be humbling because it has shown me just how wrong I can be about so many things so often. Therefore, a life in sales achieves a balance of sorts, with a prejudice towards the positive.

My book is a guide, not a manual.; be guided accordingly and believe in what you want in your own way and in your own time.

Sales works for me; my sincerest wish is that it works for you.

© Results Through Focus, LLC 2023
A. Berg, *Sales on the Go*, Business Guides on the Go,
https://doi.org/10.1007/978-1-0716-3211-6

CPSIA information can be obtained
at www.ICGtesting.com
Printed in the USA
BVHW030722300523
665074BV00017B/5